My Life's Story

How I Found Love and a Meaningful Life in Fresno
By Mike Rhodes
July 2018

Introduction

I have written My Life's Story following a diagnosis of 4th stage lung cancer in January 2018. It is now July 2018, which is longer than I thought I might live after getting the news. The doctors were not very optimistic and eventually said I might have a year to live. The cancer had spread to my brain, lymph system and bone. The doctors moved aggressively to confront the cancer, first targeting the bone with radiation therapy. The cancer had spread from my lungs to some of the bones in my spine and pelvis. They seemed particularly concerned with a bone on my upper spine, in the neck area. The problem would have been if the cancer had destroyed the bone and damaged the nerves, I might loose control of my arms and presumably other parts of my body. Fortunately, the radiation treatment worked and the neurosurgeon I was working with has told me that things seem to be healing.

The next area of concern was the brain and I did several weeks of full brain radiation. That resulted in the skin on my head getting sunburnt, cracked and my hair falling out. I was a little surprised at my reaction at first. I was not too excited about going outside with a bald head and neck brace. Which is odd. I realized that I did not want to be seen by others as anything other than the healthy person I have always been. I found that I had a bit of vanity hidden somewhere in the back of my mind, but I got over it.

Kaiser also did some genetic testing on the cancer and my body and realized that I would be eligible for a new class of drugs that help the immune system fight the cancer. The medication, given by an IV drip once every three weeks works by strengthening your immune system and making it possible for it to identify the cancer. It is different from traditional chemo therapy in the sense that it does not just kill your cells (good and bad), but it targets the cancer. The results of an MRI and CAT scan in June 2018 indicate that the cancer in my brain can no longer be seen (although it could still be there - just not big enough to see) and that the size of the cancer in my lung and lymph nodes has been reduced. That is great news!

At this time, I feel better than I thought I would, when first given the diagnosis. Yes, there are some minor side effects from the immunotherapy and radiation, but I'm not in any pain and I have lots of energy - enough to write this book and keep up with my three year old grandson.

I decided to write My Life's Story a month or two after I realized I might not have very long to live. At first I was just thinking that it would be something that I would enjoy doing and that my family would like reading the story. I know that I would have loved to read my grandparents or great grandparents life stories.

After my mom fell and broke her hip in January 2015 I spent a lot of time with her as she recovered. One of the things we did was to go through her dozens of photo albums which prompted her to talk about different things that happened in her life. I ended up producing a book with lots of photos about my mom's life. I think that experience helped push me in the direction of writing this book.

In the process of writing this book I have told friends about it and many of them have expressed an interest in reading it. I was a little surprised by the interest and honored that people outside of my immediate family would have an interest in knowing more about what makes me tick. My hope is that everyone reading this book will learn something new - I know that writing it has helped me to better understand myself.

One of the first things I thought about after realizing I was not going to live forever was how satisfied I am with my life. I really don't have anything I have to do, there are no new travel destinations I have to get to, or anything like that. What I realized is that my life had turned out really well, actually better than I could ever have imagined.

I have traveled the world, am part of a loving family, my health has been great (up until a couple of months ago) and we are financially secure. The work I have done has improved this community, I feel appreciated by my friends and have a positive outlook for the future. Life is good.

One of the first projects I embarked on when I got the diagnosis was to purge unnecessary things I have accumulated over the years. How many 10 year old computers do you really need cluttering up your garage? I read The Gentle Art of Swedish Death Cleaning, a book that convinced me that it is as important for your own mental health to clear out unneeded junk as it is for the people you will leave behind. Who wants to leave that burden on the people you love? Decluttering your life is the right thing to do and it will be appreciated by everyone you leave behind. Also, don't forget to update your Will, have a medical directive in the hands of your doctor and family and that you have a Durable Power of Attorney on file.

The story will be told in a chronological order, but because telling an episode of my life will sometimes span several years, you will find that there are a few things that seem out of sequence. I hope that is not too distracting.

While writing this book, the following quote jumped out at me: "You live only as long as the last person who remembers you." That was the theme of the movie Coco and a version of it appeared in the HBO series Westworld (Season 2, episode 10). Even though I didn't plan on this book being a quest for immortality (I have no such loft intentions), I do hope it will help you better understand the purposeful and enjoyable life I have had.

Chapter 1.....................The Foundation of my life's story
Chapter 2.....................The 1950's and early 60's
Chapter 3.....................High school days
Chapter 4.....................Why I moved to Canada
Chapter 5.....................Learning to print and Millbrook school
Chapter 6.....................How I met the love of my life
Chapter 7.....................The late 70's and early 80's
Chapter 8.....................Central America solidarity work in the 80's
Chapter 9.....................Simone is born and we transition into the 90's
Chapter 10....................The origin of the Community Alliance
Chapter 11....................I get arrested for the first time
Chapter 12....................The homeless class action lawsuit
Chapter 13....................World travel
Chapter 14....................Our daughters get married

Chapter 1

Many of the things that influenced my development as an adult happened at an early age. Some people might argue that we are who we are because of our parents, grandparents and extended family. If that is true, and I think there is some truth in it, to understand me you have to know something about my family history.

I have been interested in my family history for the last 20 or 30 years (probably going back to the mid 1990's). I'm not sure why, but I never thought very much about it before that. I'm sure that some percentage of who I am began with my families origin. If you want to see my family tree and Genealogy, I have a chart at Ancestry (dot) com that will tell you more than you want to know. Here is a link to my Family Tree:

https://www.ancestry.com/family-tree/tree/75922837/

At that website you will find a lot of details about my ancestors, photos of them, documents about their lives etc. For someone who always felt (more or less) self aware about who I am, I think I really missed some important information before discovering my family history. I also did a DNA test with Ancestry (dot) com that has reveled a lot of interesting things about my family. For example, we discovered that my mom has a sister that she did not know about. I also found that I have a half brother that I did not know about. If you decide to test your DNA, go into it with your eyes wide open. You never know what you will find.

It seems so obvious to me now that what led to my birth had to have an influence on my life. The circumstances of my mom and dad's life had a direct impact on shaping who I am. The fact that my dads family came to California from Oklahoma, were farm laborers (like something out of The Grapes of Wrath) matters. Following the Rhodes family back to North Carolina and Virginia in the 1700's has a less direct influence, but nonetheless it is foundational in determining who I am.

On my mom's side of the family, there were two distinct histories. Her dad's family (the Judd's) came from a rural area near Birmingham, England. Several brothers and sisters traveled to the Fresno area in the

1890's and started farming. The Bopp's (my maternal grandmother's family) are Volga River Germans. There are lots of books, videos etc about the immigrants who came here from the Volga River in Russia.

For more information about that side of my family, you can contact the American Historical Society of Germans from Russia - Central California Chapter at 3233 North West Ave, Fresno Ca 93705. I can't imagine that some of that history is not embedded in my DNA.

I did a second DNA test through Helix and the National Geographic. The purpose of that test was to look at our family origin, going back thousands of years. It tracks when my family lines (both male and female) left Africa and ended up in Fresno California. I thought an interesting discovery with that test was that I have 1.5% Neanderthal in me. The average is 1.3%, which I guess makes me above average (ha, ha).

So, that whole boiling cauldron of ancient family history is I'm sure influential in who I am and it is as interesting as hell to figure out where we came from, but that is not really the purpose of this book. If I live another ten years. . . maybe I will write that story.

I can trace my interest in my family history to a retreat I attended, organized by the Pan Valley Institute. Participants at the retreat were asked about their cultural heritage and there were lots of interesting stories about life in Latin America, Asia and other places around the world. I was at a loss to tell the group about my family and their cultural practices.

I simply did not know the rich history of my immigrant family and how I was a part of that story. I now know some of the stories about how my family got to Fresno, what it was like where they came from and that makes me feel a lot more connected with the world.

Henry Judd (born 1840) and Harriet Dale (born 1838). They are my great great grandparents. This is the oldest photo our family has. The photo below shows the Judd family working on a farm near Birmingham, England.

I found this photo of the Judd family working at the Kettlehouse Farm in Kingstanding (near Birmingham) at a library archive. It was taken in the early 1920's. From left to right are George Judd, his daughters Gertrude and Elsie, and his cousin Harry Judd.

Mary Mayo - she is my great grandmother.

This is my great grandfather Henry Judd shortly after he came to Fresno.

Here are some of the Bopp family in about 1931. Starting from Left to right with the adults in the back row: Harold Stump, Elsie Bopp, Marian and Henry Bopp and my grandmother Birdie. The children in the front row are Lorene Bopp, Marilyn Bopp and Beverly Judd (my aunt).

This is the Rhodes Family in 1938 shortly after they arrived in California from Oklahoma. The adults are my grandfather Frank, who I have never met and grandmother Mattie. Back row: John (my dad), Kenny and Delmar. Front Row: Frank, Mattie and Jack. Billy is in the front.

This is my great grandfather and grandmother Henry and Katie Bopp.

If you want to understand the migration from Oklahoma to California, read this book. It gives a lot of insight into why the Rhodes family moved to California.

Chapter 2

My mom says that when I was born my dad was in the Army on the East Coast. New Jersey. He flew to Fresno to be with us when I was born and was able to stay for a few days. For the first few months my mom and I lived with her folks. When my dad was discharged it did not take long for him to move us down to Los Angeles, where some of his brothers lived and he could get a job. My mom says I was 5 months old when we moved to L.A.

I don't remember much of anything about that time. The only memory that I have is being on a Hollywood movie set. My dad delivered rentals to the studios, which gave us access. I might have been about 2 years old and remember some of the indoor sets. They were filming Lassie (a show about a dog) and there was sand and a desert scene right inside the studio. I remember meeting Lassie. I think we also watched a scene they shot with Ozzie and Harriet, but that is less a memory and perhaps more of something I was told about.

When we moved back to Fresno we lived in the Projects (public housing) about a block or so from Edison High School. Within a year, we moved to the Pleasant Avenue house. I was about 3 years old. I can remember walking through the house before it was completed. The house was on the last block in a suburb at the edge of town. There was nothing beyond our house except farmland. Looking from our kitchen window you could see peach trees, fig trees and down the street were Thompson Seedless grapes and a large open irrigation ditch. Perfect for young kids to run wild.

The neighborhood was a pretty nice place to grow up. As we moved in they were building Wilson Elementary School at Ashlan and Hughes, easy walking distance from our house. I was in one of the first Kindergarten classes when it opened. By the time I got through Wilson they had built Cooper Jr High, right at the end of our street.

The real pleasure of growing up where I did was that there were a lot of kids my age in the neighborhood. Since I was an only child, that was cool. Some of the neighborhood kids became like brothers and sisters. The other thing is that there were miles and miles of open land - well, a lot of farm land but space to roam. The first year or two I don't think I roamed all that much, but eventually me and my friends got to know the lay of the land pretty well. By the time I was ten I probably knew every nook and cranny in a 1 or 2 mile circumference.

The place I grew up in had its own special beauty too. In the spring the tree blossoms were fantastic. You could hear the frogs (thousands of them) croaking every night from the irrigation ditch. The Sierra Nevada mountains could be seen year round, so you knew you were in a valley. Now, if you see the snow capped mountains after a storm you are lucky.

The 1950's was also about spending time with family. For me, that meant holidays with the grand and great grandparents, aunts, uncles and my cousin. We spent time together by cooking BBQ's and other things.

Mostly, or I should say almost entirely, I'm speaking here about my mom's family. My mom and dad were separated in the mid 50's and they were divorced a few years later.   Unfortunately, that resulted in an almost complete separation from my dad's side of the family.

I think the end of their marriage was largely due to his drinking and going out with other women. My mom told me recently that the final straw for her was when he came home, hit her and then turned his wrath on me. I thank her for protecting me (I might have been 3 or 4 at the time). Given those circumstances it was probably a good idea for them to divorce.

Growing up as an only child, with a single mom, in suburban Fresno during the 1950's was a big part of my life. My mom always worked. She was a telephone operator and when she was at work she had a neighbor look after me. That mostly worked out, but I had a lot of time on my hands. As I got older I spent time playing with the neighborhood kids, exploring the outside boundary of our world. I was in the cub scouts, I spent a lot of time staying with neighbors and watching some TV.

The difference between television today and what was available 60 years ago is like night and day. There were only a few channels available, for a long time it was just black and white, everything was broadcast (from a tower in the Sierras) and after a certain hour the TV station shut down for the night. I remember the Bee (Scoopy - the mascot for the Fresno Bee, Ch 24 and KMJ) would fly onto the screen at the end of the day, say goodnight and then there would just be a test pattern until the morning.

My cousin Nat and his family must have moved to Fresno sometime in the mid to late 50's. He and I had a complicated relationship. We had very different personalities and preferences. He was often times getting into trouble and was eager to draw me into his adventures. I was a pretty introspective and easy going child. It was a somewhat unnatural mash up.

I'll give an example. When Nat came over to visit, with his mom and dad, we were left to play together. I might have been 3. Nat would have been 4 or 5. Parents in those days did not hover and over protect their kids. I had a wagon and some little golf clubs. Nat said he was going to teach me to golf. I thought that was great. I sat in the wagon with a golf club, Nat pulled the wagon and one of our parents took a photo of the cute boys heading off to play golf. We go down about two houses and stop. I have one golf club and my cousin has another. He points out a tree (newly planted by the city in a neighbors yard) and he tells me to chop it down. Of course, I chopped the tree down. The neighbors were not happy about it. They came down and yelled at our parents. Nat thought it was hilarious. I was confused about the situation.

Eventually, I caught on to what it meant to hang out with my big cousin, but did not have the skill to manage him. I usually just tagged along and participated in whatever mayhem he would lead me into. I'm not writing this to be critical of Nat. This is about me. I didn't have to do what he did, but I followed along because I didn't know what else to do and I didn't have any strong male role models.

Fortunately, as we got older, we never got into any real trouble. Nat did, but not with me. As I got older (was it 11 or 12?) I started to realize that I needed to keep a little distance and be cautious about how far I would go along with the chaos that would result from each visit.

I could go into detail about what might have driven my cousin to his state of mind, but that would be too long of a detour and is probably a tale better told by him.

That said, I did get into some trouble on my own, or at least with other kids in the neighborhood. I was no angel. When they started building homes in the fields across the street, a friend of mine and I did some serious monkey wrenching (sabotage something, especially as a form of protest). Billy and I would go to the construction site after they were done for the day and literally tear walls down. We were probably 10 at the time. We never got caught, but it got so close one time that we pulled back from the abyss. Billy also would go to stores with me and he would steal comic books and things like that. I thought that was pretty bold.

The reason we did damage to the new homes was because the developers had torn down what we considered to be our playground. Technically it was a fig and peach orchard, but we considered that to be our domain and were really pissed that we would not be able to climb trees and roam about in the orchards.

During the 50's and early 60's my mom and I would go on vacations around the state. We went to Santa Cruz, where her brother lived, we went to the Sierra's and up to the Gold Country. I think those were pretty happy times. When I got to be 12 or 13 I was no longer as good of company so we had to make some adjustments. I don't think there was anything unusual going on, just the usual adolescent nonsense that just about everyone goes through.

John Rhodes (my dad), Vie (my mom) and me looking perfectly happy to be sitting on their laps.

Me and my mom shortly after moving into the house on Pleasant. I was about three years old when we moved there.

These are some of the kids in the neighborhood. I'm on the far left, my cousin Nat is next to me. The girl in the back row next to my cousin is Paula, then Val, Yvonne and Earl. My dog Pepper Pot got in the shot. I'm not sure about the kid in the front row.

Me and my friend Yvonne Pottet. My mom worked at the phone company with Betty, Yvonne's mom. I spent a lot of time at their house. I think this might be us on our first day of school.

From left to right: Johnny (my uncle), Vie, me, Birdie (my grandmother) and John (my grandfather). I guess we drove up into the Sierra Mountains that day to play in the snow.

Mike and cousin Nat just before they went two doors down and chopped down the neighbors tree.

Chapter 3

When I moved on to Jr. High School I became more aware of the social stratification, class and racial division that was taking place. The world was not as happy of a place with a lot of my peers jockeying for position and some people just left behind. I tried to avoid the rat race, but that is impossible. Young guys at that time in their lives can be very aggressive and there were a lot of rivalries and sometimes those led to fights.

There was this guy that wanted to provoke a fight with me and it ended up being an after school fight that it seemed as if half the school wanted to watch. We walked out of the school and to the ally across the street. We got about half way down and he just turns around and hits me in the nose. Shit! I fought back and everyone was excited to have a real fight on their hands. We beat each other up pretty good, but nobody yielded. Finally, it was clear there was not going to be a winner. Since he was socially ranked above me, I considered that a win. After the fight, I really didn't have another incident like that.

The other thing is that I was damn good at wrestling. Yeah, who knew? But, I kind of kicked butt in about the 8th grade in PE, mostly due to my wrestling skill. Other than that, Jr. High was pretty non eventful.

Fresno High was 10th, 11th and 12 grade. High school for me started in September of 1967 where I was thrown in with a whole bunch of kids from other schools that I didn't know. I took the bus back and forth to school. Politically and socially things were starting to shift, with the Vietnam War, drugs and rock and roll.

Everyone more or less falls in with a group of like minded schoolmates and I was no different. Our group thought of ourselves as being outside of the mainstream. We couldn't see where we were going, but we were attracted to the counter culture that was starting to emerge. Was it the music, the drugs or anti-war politics that drove us forward? Probably all of that and more. Also, we just had a good time together and our friendships were an affirmation of our emerging world view - which for me was questioning authority, opposing the war, going to as many rock concerts as possible and enjoying time with friends.

What was it that I experienced that sent me down such a radically different path than most of my peers? For a long time I have identified the horrific war in Vietnam as being the trigger that sent me on a journey looking for deeper answers. As a young man who might be drafted I choose to look deeply into the underlying causes of the war. I thought that if I was going to be drafted and sent to a war, that I might die in, I wanted to know why.

What I learned in that search for the truth molded my thinking for years to come. I found that the Vietnam war, as explained by the powers that be, painted a very one sided picture. The war, government spokespeople said, was about containing Communism, stopping the aggressive North Vietnamese and defending democracy.

The reality was something all together different. Our country was the aggressor in the war, lied about things as basic as what started the war, was engaged in bombing innocent civilians and was upholding a dictator. I tried to look at things from the point of view of the Vietnamese and realized that, in many ways, I had more in common with them than the imperialistic, exploitive and capitalistic architects of this nations ruling class.

A key factor in the evolution of my thinking was the ability to empathize and see things from someone else's perspective. I saw the Vietnamese people fighting for their countries independence, similar to the War of Independence we fought against England. That would put us on the wrong side of history - fighting for U.S. corporations right to extract natural resources from Vietnam, defend the puppet we installed as a dictator, and being a pawn in the Cold War. And. . . I was going to fight and die for that? I don't think so!

I was shocked by how so many people would allow themselves to be drafted and go to a war, in which we were clearly on the wrong side. I just didn't feel like I shared the same values as many of my classmates and the people running this country. They wrapped themselves in the flag and in their telling of the story, they were the patriots. A common slogan was "America, Love it or Leave it." The divide was summed up in a sitcom that came out in the early 1970's - All in the Family. On the one hand you had the racist blue collar Archie Bunker attacking his daughter and her husband who were against the war and in support of economic and social justice. It was kind of painful to watch, but it did put its finger on the divide in the country at that time.

If my opposition to the war in Vietnam was the only thing going on, my life might have gone in a different direction. But, the emergence of a significant counter culture movement, music and mind altering drugs like LSD were all happening at the same time. That convergence put me in a group of people at my High School who looked at things differently from what we called the establishment. The rejection of mainstream cultural norms and the hope for a future of peace, social and economic justice set us apart from many of our peers. At least I thought that we shared that dream. But, as time has gone by, many of my high school friends have drifted decidedly to the right. Some of them are Republicans who think Trump is a great guy. So, there has to be some kind of a misperception of reality on my part to think we were all on the same page.

The other explanation is that people change over time. My life experiences led me to a world view where I hold progressive values and it is likely that many of my high school friends took different twists and turns that led them to where they are today. I think it is really hard to grow up in this country, surrounded by things like Fox news, racism, sexism, classism, patriarchy, relentless competition and the alienation that comes from working hard but never getting ahead. If that is your reality it can lead to identifying with and ideologically agreeing with the oppressor in a hope to get ahead.

This quote by Steve Biko says it best: "The most potent weapon in the hands of the oppressor is the mind of the oppressed."

That said, I still find it hard to understand how someone you were close to, dropped acid with, listened to the Grateful Dead with, can end up voting for Donald Trump. But, hey - we are not going to figure that out here, so I will just note the fact and leave it at that.

The social and political separation from students not a part of our movement for change had a profound impact on my thinking. I always felt like an outsider to those who were conservative and had been elected to political office and controlled the economy. Therefore, I did not see the value of vying for power or working on politics from inside of the system. It made more sense to me that the youth and counter culture were going to create an entirely new and more egalitarian system that would replace the corrupt and decaying establishment.

It is hard to describe today how hopeful we were at the time. We were certain that we would succeed in ending the war and creating a new society based on our values. We had momentum and maybe it was my youthful idealism, but I seriously thought the old guard would crumble under its own contradictions. There was an anti-materialist aspect to my thinking - the idea that we (as a society) could live better with less. That we could be in harmony with our environment and that would lead to a more fulfilling and sustainable life. This corresponded to an appreciation of Native American culture - how they were able to live here for thousands of years without destroying the environment.

In retrospect I think that to some extent, this view of wanting to reduce our footprint on the planet was easier for me to contemplate than it would be for someone who was even poorer than I was. There were a lot of people that just wanted to get ahead, not worry about if they were going to eat today and I was telling them to be less materialistic. That probably didn't like a good idea to a lot of people.

My concern was that conservatives and the establishment were destroying the earth by trying to dominate and control our natural environment, rather than working in harmony and looking at what the impact would be 50, 100 or even 200 years from now.

I have come to believe that this is a fundamental difference between progressive environmentalists and the right wing conservatives that believe God put "man" on earth to have domination over all of the plants, animals, rivers and other natural features on this planet. I see it differently. I think that we are all interconnected and that unless we figure out how to live in harmony with our environment we will be in for some difficult times ahead.

There were other currents of thought taking place at the same time. I felt pretty fatalistic about the nuclear arms race and believed that it was likely that a confrontation with the Soviet Union would lead to a cataclysmic war. That idea ran in a completely contradictory direction from the hopefulness of the youth counter culture which had hopes of moving the country in a new direction. And, other than demonstrating against the insanity of building more nuclear weapons, it didn't seem like this was something we (the youth) had control over.

Those of us who shared the values of the counter culture hung out together at school, the guys and a lot of the young women had long hair, dressed differently and had alternative events (like rock concerts) that were the center of our world. We were clearly the minority, but had enough critical mass and cohesion to feel like we were a part of a movement for change.

There was another element that held this group of young people together that is a little more challenging to explain, given what has happened over the last 50 years. Drugs were looked at differently in the late 1960's than they are today. Drugs were different in the 60's and early 70's than they are today. Marijuana was much less potent than it is today. The high was mellow and not as psychoactive. It was used when we got together as a social lubricant, perhaps like a glass of wine or two is looked at today. The group I hung out with used marijuana, maybe drank a little wine or beer, but hard drugs like heroin were pretty much unknown to us. Although, as time moved forward we started experimenting with some psychedelic drugs like LSD, mushrooms etc.

I first used marijuana in the summer of 1969. I remember the date because my cousin and I went to Yosemite in August and camped out in the meadows. It was there that people were talking about this big rock concert that was going to take place in a week or so in Woodstock, New York. We briefly considered going, but we did not have the resources to get there. Instead, we got high and moved on, driving to Monterrey the next day.

I think that the use of marijuana and later LSD influenced my thinking outside the box. Up until that time (when I was 15 or 16) I had been living a pretty mainstream life in the suburbs of a mid-sized town in the Central Valley. Most of the things I would encounter in my environment, school and family never pushed the boundaries of conventional thought. When I started smoking marijuana and hanging out with friends who did, it became obvious that there was something going on beyond what I had been exposed to. Of course, a part of that expanded universe was the Hippie phenomena, the anti-war movement and the experimentation with psychedelic drugs.

I became a vegetarian during this time, not eating meat for health, environmental, economic and humanitarian reasons. I remained a vegetarian until I went to Cuba in December of 1977.

To digress just a bit I want to say a few words about my early Jr. High and High School days. I was a mediocre student at best. I had no motivation to do well and my family made no demands on me, other than they expected me to finish high school. So, I did what was expected of me. . . which was very little. That is actually one regret that I have. If I had that to do over again I would have found a way to make learning interesting and got on a track that led me to college. With more skill, knowledge, and networking I might have been able to have accomplished more than I did.

I talked to my mom recently (in 2016) about those days. I know she did not like school and she really could see no reason why anyone would torture themselves by going to school any longer than they had to. She never seriously considered going to college, even though she had good grades and was smart. She literally just wanted to get out of high school, get married and have a family. She did not expect to work at a job for a living, but that is what happened.

I was surprised that my mom wanted to have more children and had planned to buy a bigger house to accommodate the growing family. And all of this time I thought that she just wanted to be a single mother and raise me.

My mom wanted me to have enough skill and schooling so I could get a job and survive in the world. She even suggested that I might want to work at AT&T as a a telephone operator. While I think my mom liked her job, mostly because in was not too hard or stressful and had flexible hours, she didn't see the work someone did as being what they really liked to do.

In that conversation with my mom, I told her that it was my opinion that someone could gain the skills and knowledge they need to get a job they enjoyed and were good at doing by going to college. I said that if I had done better in high school that I might have continued my education, learned more about journalism and got a job I really liked. And, the people

I would have met might have helped me get a job as a journalist or a photographer.

This is probably an issue my mom and I disagree on, but that is OK. Mostly my mom and I get along, we agree on most political and social issues. The fact that she did not push me to go to college is water under the bridge and not something I think about these days. I'm not even sure that if my mom pushed me to go to college I would have gone.

When I did get through High School, because of my attitude, I could hardly spell, reading was difficult and I lacked a lot of basic information and skills that most people take for granted. It was a very challenging road from near illiteracy to becoming the editor of a local newspaper.

The way I looked at high school at the time when I was a senior was that it (the educational system) wanted to turn out workers that the "establishment" would use for fodder in their wars and as cogs in their factories to make a corrupt system function. Did I want to be a part of that? Hell no! I wanted to be a part of the cultural and social revolution, that was already in progress.

To put it mildly, I would say I was alienated in High School. My friends and I dressed differently, we thought differently and were (by and large) happy to be outside of the usual activities the other students were doing. For us, going to rock concerts, anti-war demonstrations and experimenting with drugs was what we were interested in and what built a sense of community for us. The "straight" students had their school dances, football games etc.

That distrust I had for the establishment would, in many ways, follow me into adulthood. For example, the War Against Drugs was pretty intense at the time (the late 60's and early 70's). Most of my friends, therefore did not trust the police, because they wanted to take away something that we considered a socially bonding herb. Our group, you might call it our tribe, had social cohesion and would use marijuana when we got together and had fun. The fact that we were under attack by the police gave me a serious mistrust of what they were up to. That reservation extended to my being very cautious about people who would cooperate with the police to entrap our friends and have them arrested. I carried that basic mistrust of the police and hostility toward snitches with me for many years.

The existence of an alternative world view was a powerful motivating factor in getting me to do some critical thinking about what was going on and what I wanted to do with my life. That alternative and the threat of being drafted to fight in the Vietnam War got me thinking long and hard about my life. I came to the conclusion that we were wrong to uphold a dictator in South Vietnam, lie about the origin of the war and send this countries youth to kill the people of Vietnam who were fighting for their freedom and liberation. That understanding, when I was still a senior in high school, led me to not register for the draft. That act alone made me an outlaw and I realized I could spend a significant amount of time in prison for my convictions. The threat of arrest and imprisonment further alienated me from this country.

Criminalizing the youth because they supported peace, demanded the truth about the war and had enough convictions to resist the draft was wrong. I always believed that I was being patriotic for standing up for what I believed in and was disappointed that many of my peers allowed themselves to get caught up in the system. I believe that what you do matters and that by saying no to the war by risking arrest makes a strong statement.

This line of thinking also led to me having a more cynical view of this country, because I thought "if they are lying about the war in Vietnam, what else are they lying about?" I became interested in UFO's, conspiracy theories like the John Kennedy assassination and ideas about how this country was manipulated by a ruling elite. Once there was that breakdown and I knew our government was lying about one thing (like the Vietnam War), I wanted to know what else we were being mislead about.

I came to believe that even though I was born in this country, that did not obligate me to blindly agree with all policies, wars and economic dictates. I opposed fist pumping nationalism and saw that as one of the root causes of America's path that led to the Vietnam War. Furthermore, I saw the Vietnam War as being an extension of the Cold War, which is predicated on the right of capitalists to exploit the working class. The Socialist/ Communist alternative of cooperation and equality actually appealed to me more. I felt that this country, because of its basic belief in the capitalist system and use of the military, would end up time and again on the wrong side of history. Defending dictators, attacking workers and trying to stop people struggling for independence, liberation, social and economic justice. For some strange reason, I wanted to be on the right side of history.

I would later learn more about how the US overthrew foreign governments by supporting opposition groups, creating economic chaos and manipulating the electoral process. The US would use any tool to accomplish their goals - torture, murder, upholding brutal dictators, economic warfare and if it was deemed necessary direct intervention through military action.

In the end, I decided I would leave America and move to another country. I think the first time this occurred to me was when I was outside of Fresno High, during an anti-war demonstration. My career guidance advisor walked by, saw me participating in the protest, grabbed and dragged me into his office. He was seriously pissed that I was not in class, but instead protesting the Vietnam War. He was Armenian and told me about their history of genocide and used that as an argument for why I should support the war (because the U.S. gave Armenians a place to escape to). I argued back that if he was drafted and forced to go to Armenia and fight against his own people, would he do it? I told him I would rather leave the country than to fight in an unjust war, killing people who have never done anything to hurt me. While my argument had no apparent effect on him, it did convince me to consider leaving the U.S.

At first I thought that after I graduated that I would buy a VW van and drive south, maybe ending up somewhere in South America. After looking at maps, reading about some of the history and realizing that I had done really bad in my Spanish class, I reconsidered my choice of destinations. Canada seemed like a much more likely destination. They speak English, they are a little more socially and politically progressive than we are and there was an infrastructure for people like me to relocate in Canada.

The path that led me to Canada in 1971.

During the last 1/2 of my senior year at Fresno High I became involved in what was known as The Resistance in Fresno. The Resistance was what was generally considered the heart of the anti-war movement, but in reality the analysis behind that group went beyond the single issue of war and peace. There was a whole alternative lifestyle aspect to The Resistance.

Many of the core members lived in communes (houses or land where multiple individuals and families lived) and collectively made decisions. We generally looked at ending the war in Vietnam as being connected to other changes that were needed in this country - like environmental sustainability, growing and eating organic food, women's rights and a sense of economic justice (like supporting the farmworkers and their union, the UFW). I would describe my politics at the time as being anarchistic. I totally rejected the mainstream political landscape (Democrat/Republican) and felt that a much deeper and fundamental change was needed. Everyone in our family, as far as I know, were Democrats. I was always told that the Democrats supported working peoples interests and the Republicans favored the elite. With both parties supporting the war in Vietnam, I was unconvinced that I wanted anything to do with those two parties.

About the closest I came to electoral political activism was that I supported most of the goals of the Peace and Freedom Party. I even considered running for the Fresno City Council at one time. I took out nomination papers and gave serious consideration to running. I remember the owner of a health food store, upon hearing of my interest in running, took out his wallet and offered me (what I considered at the time) a lot of money. Eventually, I decided not to run, because I believed (probably correctly) that my politics were so far outside of the mainstream in Fresno that I knew I didn't have a chance in hell of winning. I was not yet ready to spend my time arguing with people about my vision for what needed to be done to end the war, stop the drug war and have a sustainable environment and economic justice.

Also, at about this time, I had what I would now describe as an interest in spirituality. This started out at about the time when I was in high school during my senior year. I decided to move out of my mom's house in December of 1969 and rent an apartment with a group of friends. The apartment was a couple of blocks from Fresno High, so I continued going to school during the day and enjoying the freedom of not living at my mom's house.

The experience of living on my own had a profound impact on me. At first, it was just a big non stop party. Everybody came to our place after school to hang out and get high. At the time, I was selling marijuana (small amounts), amphetamines and sometimes LSD to pay the rent. It seemed like a perfectly reasonable thing to do at the time, but now it looks like a point in time when my life might have spun out of control. Instead, I started looking at what I was doing and where I wanted to go in my life. The drug use at our apartment was escalating - for example, one of our house mates was shooting adrenaline and starting to act pretty bizarre. I started thinking about where all of this drug use and lifestyle was heading and turned in a new and unexpected direction.

This new direction took the form of what I would describe as a spiritual journey. At first I thought Christianity would be the answer and thought by following those teachings, it would lead to a better life. I wanted some kind of structure for a path forward that would lead to a world more in harmony with what I saw as sustainable. One thing that I did, that I'm sure really pissed some people off, was I took the vial of adrenaline and dropped it off at a hospital. I know, that was a rather odd thing to do, but I saw the shooting of that drug as doing more harm than good and that (at least in my mind) justified the action. Needless to say, my housemates disagreed and the living arrangement collapsed. Within a month one of the people who rented the house with me committed suicide. He was the one shooting the adrenaline.

My spirituality soon moved beyond Christianity and I found myself studying eastern religion, reading the Bhagavad Gita and books by Paramahansa Yogananda (Autobiography of a Yogi). A friend of mine, Rob Combs was into this a lot more than I was. Needless to say, this way of looking at the world did not bring me closer to mainstream America, which in my opinion was grossly materialistic and maintained its position in the world by waging wars of aggression and economic domination. So, there was this unusual combination of eastern philosophy, experimentation with mind altering drugs (mostly LSD) and anti war activism that significantly impacted the last half of my senior year in high school. Timothy Leary had a phrase that captured what I was feeling at the time. He said to "Turn on, tune in and drop out." That sounded about right to me.

Sticking with the theme of my spirituality, I will take us on a brief detour, to look at the evolution of my thinking. There was a somewhat dark aspect to the way I viewed the world at this time. On the one hand, I did have the belief that the youth could bring about massive political and social change. But, on the other hand, I thought that the situation was so awful that drastic measures needed to be taken. I looked at the Buddhist monks in

Vietnam setting themselves on fire to protest the war and I seriously thought that might be a good thing to do. If done in this country, an act of that magnitude would catch peoples attention. Obviously, I did not follow through with that idea, but it was more than just a thought that flashed through my mind. In the end, I decided there were more effective ways of working for social change.

I left most of my spiritual/religious ideas behind at about that time (in the early 70's). I came to the conclusion that no religious group had a lock on the truth. It was all based on faith. Sure, some religions could motivate their believers to do good things, but sometimes it went the other way. I also came to believe that most religion was like an opiate for the masses. In other words, religion was being used to manipulate people to do what the (system? establishment? capitalists?) wanted them to do - like fight in unjust wars, to justify this misogynist culture/society and the mindless consumerism that is all around us.

It has taken my entire lifetime to get to where I'm at on this topic, but I now see myself as an Atheist. I simply don't believe that anyone has all of the answers about why and how we are here. I understand how comforting it would be to have a belief system that came to the conclusion that there would be pie in the sky when you die, but I am not buying it.

I'm not even sure that if someone explained to me what was going on in the universe and how everything got to where it is today that I would understand. I suspect that exercise would be like my trying to explain physics to an ant. I don't know if we are capable of understand what the universe is about, even if it could be explained by someone who had all of the answers. I think that the complexity of it is beyond our understanding, although I don't think that should stop us from trying.

In the final analysis I'm fine with not knowing. There are a lot of things I don't know about, the meaning of the universe and our place in it is a big deal, but I can accept that my knowledge of things is limited. I think that is better than making something up and presenting it as gospel.

Returning back to the late 1960's and early 1970's.

Leary's comment (turn on, tune in and drop out) left me a little conflicted. While I really enjoyed getting high, I could see that it was seriously impacting my life. The pot left me unmotivated to do very much outside of that culture and the psychedelics sent my mind in ever more unorthodox directions. The other factor that led me to seriously consider cutting back on my drug intake was the relationship that I had with my father.

My dad never played a significant role in my life and as I grew older I realized that his alcoholism was largely responsible for our lack of bonding. When I was young, he would take me for a few days a year, but even then he would not spend quality time with me. I remember the times he would leave me in the car while he was drinking in a bar - it seemed like such a tragic missed opportunity. He could have built a relationship with me, but he had other priorities. The point at which I came to the conclusion that I really didn't want to hang out with him was in about 1970 when he got me a job in Bakersfield. We stayed in a hotel and worked on a construction project (probably working on a freeway or some other road work). I was assigned some rather meaningless job like holding a sign telling people to stop and then to drive slow through the construction zone. When we were done working, my dad would drop me off at the hotel and go out drinking. I would read something like the Bhagavad Gita (which I'm sure he thought was just insane) and he would get shit faced drunk. There was no effort whatsoever by him to get to know me. The final straw was him coming back to the room so drunk he could not find the bathroom and he pissed on the wall. That was it for me. From that time forward I had no interest in spending time with him. It was worse than being mad at him, I just no longer had any desire to get to know him. It also led me to realize that drug/alcohol addiction could have serious down sides and that I did not want to be like my dad. That was a significant and transformative realization, which led to my cutting way back on drugs and in my decision to have meaningful relationships with my children, should I ever have any.

My mom was pretty easy going about raising me, which I liked. She never objected to my going to rock concerts, protesting the war or anything else. That all seemed reasonable to me, even if some of my other friends were at war with their families about doing some of the same things.

How did this play out in my teenage years? Well, I would travel to S.F. to see bands, like Led Zeppelin. I hitchhiked to the Altamont Rock Concert (the West Coast answer to Woodstock) to see the Rolling Stones and a bunch of other bands.

In August of 1969 my uncle Johnny died in an automobile accident in Santa Cruz. He had moved there several years earlier, had a wife and two children - Julie and Janet (my cousins). This was a big deal as my mom really loved Johnny and he was everything to John and Birdie (my grandparents).

June 1967 - Mike graduated from Cooper Jr High. If you look close enough, you might be able to see a hint of "attitude" on that happy graduates face. I don't think I liked the clip on tie.

This is my mom Vie and me, probably in about 1968

The most potent weapon in the hands of the oppressor is the mind of the oppressed

Steve Biko

Chapter 4

My mom's sister Bev committed suicide in July 1970, about a month after I graduated. That event really upset my mom (understandably so). I had briefly moved to Half Moon Bay after graduating from high school, but when Bev died I moved back to Fresno.

Back in Fresno my focus was to save enough money so I could move out of the country. I bought a 1 ton used step van from the post office and converted it into a mobil home. I got several jobs in unskilled work places. One was in a crafts shop where I made (along with 20 or 30 other people) resin balls that were used in various products. It was incredibly dangerous work with little or no safety regulations. Workers would pass out because of the fumes from the resin and lack of ventilation. Workers using drill presses would have the drills break all of the time, flying into various parts of their unprotected bodies. I worked there and at other equally dangerous places so I could save enough money to move to Canada.

My decision to move to Canada reflected my determination not to cooperate with the US government. I did not register for the draft, because I thought my participation would suggest that I was validating the government's right to send young people to war. I wanted to make it perfectly clear that I totally rejected their system. At the same time, I did not think that I deserved to go to jail. I wanted to move away to a more enlightened country where I could contribute what I had to give. Canada was sympathetic with the US anti-war movement and accepted about 30,000 young men who left the U.S to avoid the draft.

It is interesting to note (I had no idea of this at the time) that the Bopp side of my family (my maternal grandmother's family) had left the Volga River region in Russia and came to Fresno, in part because the Russians were starting to draft the young men in their villages. There had been an agreement when the Germans moved to the Volga River region that they would NOT have to serve in the Russian military.

One life altering realization I had at about this time was that I rejected the Patriarchal model of the family. I never had any strong male role models, I was raised by a single mom and did not like the hierarchical model that was common at the time. My dad was completely missing in action, my friends dads either drank to much, were not warm and compassionate and/or they worked all of the time.

With a new paradigm emerging in the counter culture of men and women being partners, sharing the work and making collective decisions, that just made so much sense to me. I did not want to be the guy who told everyone what to do, was alienated at work and drank himself into oblivion at night. I wanted to be an equal partner in a relationship, share the household work and have children that respected their parents. Not because they are afraid of them, but because everyone would be treated with dignity and mutual respect.

My girlfriend at the time was still in High School and I decided to wait until she graduated and then hit the road. The Draft Resistance had connected with sympathizers in Canada and set up a (sort of) underground railroad. I was connected with a family in Calgary, Alberta who would help me get through the immigration system by offering me a job, a place to live etc.

They didn't "actually" get me a job or find a place for me to live, but it looked good on paper. I easily got a "Landed Immigrant" status, a Canadian ID card, apartment and job.

I found Canada an interesting place to live and work, but I was also isolated from the culture and political life I was familiar with in Fresno California. Sure, I could have stayed there, lived a good life and never moved back. Things were pretty simple - you work, fit into a comfortable middle class life and then what? It was that lack of living a meaningful life that I missed. I had a job at a pizza making factory (Oh My Pizza) and got promoted, was contemplating buying a new car (the one ton van was a bit much to be driving around town in the snow and ice) when I realized that I was not going to be happy in Calgary.

I quite my job, packed and moved back to Fresno after only being gone for about 6 months. Returning to Fresno resulted in a deeper feeling of connectedness with the groups working for political and social change. I felt I had a moral obligation to do what I could to end the war in Vietnam and move this country in a new direction. So, when we moved back to Fresno I became more involved in political activity.

Beverly Barnes, Johnny Judd and Vie Rhodes. This photo was taken in front of Bev's trailer, probably when she and Ernie lived in or near San Diego.

Nore Edwards and I walking on the mall in downtown Calgary, Canada in the summer of 1971. This photo was taken by a street photographer.

NUMÉRO
D'ASSURANCE
SOCIALE

CANADA

SOCIAL
INSURANCE
NUMBER

623 348 620

MICHAEL JOHN RHODES

SIGNATURE   *Mike Rhodes*

Chapter 5

For me, the movement for change in Fresno, centered around two places - The Building and Shanti bookstore in Van Ness Village. The building was a large space that included numerous new-left groups. There were anti war groups in The Building, women's groups, an alternative newspaper (Grassroots), a food co-op and more. The Shanti bookstore sold alternative books and magazines and had a print shop in the back.

I volunteered to staff the bookstore and while doing that learned how to print, which was the skill that would define a major portion of my working life. It happened because Lang Russell, the lead printer, had a large order for fliers announcing a rally featuring Jane Fonda and Tom Hayden. Lang had to run an errand and asked me to watch the press. He showed me how to turn it on and off, add ink etc. And then, he left. It was sink or swim. Apparently I had a knack for printing and that is what launched my career as a printer. Interestingly, the press I learned on was the Multi-1250 that Joan Baez had bought for the Fresno Resistance. Ten years later I would be instrumental in sending that printing press to El Salvador, where the FMLN would use it to print literature to support the effort for peace, social and economic justice in that country.

Larry Sheehy, who owned the Shanti book store, also had a job as a janitor at the First Christian Church. He wanted to leave that job and trained me to be his replacement. That was perfect, because I could do that job in the evenings (with a flexible schedule), leaving me free during the day to do political work. Nore, my wife, (we had gotten married in Calgary), was not interested in my political activism and we grew apart.

The job at the church put me in touch with Millbrook School which was located there. Millbrook was an alternative school that allowed children to learn at their own pace and focus on what they were interested in. The Millbrook elementary school was at the church and the High School was at another location.

Eventually, my knowledge of printing (limited as it was) and proximity to Millbrook led them to offer me a job teaching printing at the High School. I thought they were crazy to ask me to teach printing, because I barely knew how to print. But, they were persuasive and I jumped on board and helped set up Millbrook Press where we taught students and did some commercial printing. We ran the shop as an autonomous collective, had pictures of Chairman Mao on the wall and enjoyed working together.

Jimmy Carter was the president at the time and offered Amnesty to anyone who had not registered for the draft. I was the first person in Fresno to take him up on the offer and the Fresno Bee wrote a big article about the event. Basically, I felt that it made no sense for me to go to prison and I was happy to have that threat lifted from over my head. I was surprised by The Bee's interest in the story and they followed me through the process of accepting the amnesty from the District Attorney and then getting processed through the Draft Board. The thing is that I would never have been drafted, because my draft number was so high (the selection process was based on your birthday and mine was 288 out of 365). I was somewhat conflicted about accepting the amnesty, but I really didn't want to go to prison, when avoiding incarceration was so easy.

Nore and I continued to go our separate ways until she was convinced that I was having an affair with someone and I moved out of the apartment we lived in. I could have convinced her that I was not having an affair (because I wasn't), but I could not think of a good reason to stay in the marriage. Within a year or so we got a divorce.

I moved into an urban commune on Fulton street (between Belmont and Divisadero) where I felt right at home. Most of the commune members (we actually had two huge houses next door to each other) worked at Millbrook. We had a huge Community Garden across the street, we worked and lived together and everyone got along. We were a big happy family.

I worked at Millbrook School for about 3 years (from 1973 - 76). At first I just taught printing, but eventually also taught other classes in the High School. Classes I taught included Nuclear Energy, which was a big issue at that time. The Diablo Canyon Nuclear Power Plant had just gone online and there were constant protests against the facility. The class I taught included background about how nuclear power was generated, what were the criticisms of it and finished with a tour of the plant by the class. The students then had the opportunity to intelligently discuss, with PG&E representatives (at the Diablo facility) their concerns about Nuclear Power.

According to the January 1976 Millbrook School catalog, here are the classes I taught:

Newspaper (how to produce your own newspaper)
Vegetarian Cooking (Yes, I was a vegetarian from 1970 - 1977)
Nuclear Energy
Alternative Energy Sources
Writing and Selling Nonfiction
The Assassination of John F Kennedy
Orienteering (which was about how to use a map and compass in the mountains)
Free Food (about Wild Edibles in Fresno County)
Printing

I was also writing during this time. The first article I ever sold was about the United Farm Workers movement to a magazine called "Engage, Social Action" which was a publication of the United Methodist Church. They paid me $150, which was enough for the rent that month. I thought that was great! Doing what you like, and people are throwing money at you! How cool is that? Eventually, I wrote and published Wild Edibles of Fresno County. Not only did I write and publish the book, I printed and distributed it too. The money I made from that book sustained me for several years. We went through 3 printings (2,500 copies), I did some public speaking about the book and it gave me some new confidence about my writing and speaking abilities.

I also constantly sent The Fresno Bee letters to the editor, which they mostly printed. There is a 3 ring binder on our book shelf that has dozens of the letters printed in the Bee. After the 70's I don't think I saved the letters I sent or what they printed. There were probably 100's of letters to the editor I wrote that they printed.

Keep in mind that when I got out of high school I was barely able to read and write and my spelling was atrocious. I had to check an album out of the library to learn how to type. But, by the early 1970's I was writing and selling articles, books and being invited to various venues as a speaker. What motivated me to learn how to become more literate was that I had something I was interested in and I wanted to share my knowledge. I wasn't stupid, but I didn't have any motivation in school to do well. In high school I thought what I was learning was meant to benefit a corrupt system that wanted to use people like me for the fodder in their wars and to fill their factories with docile and compliant workers. When I realized that education could be used to change the world, I found the motivation I needed to learn the skills needed to contribute to what I saw as a revolutionary movement.

My friend Rob Combs is on the left, a military recruiter in the middle and me on the right. This was at Fresno City College in about 1970.

Grassroots was an alternative/independent newspaper in Fresno during the early 1970's.

From left to right: Lang Russell, Richard Gillaspy, Linda Swearengin, Carol Flores and me at Millbrook Press. We are standing behind our Chief 22 press

Millbrook school offers students unique education

Self-motivation, self-criticism and self-regulation are principles on which Millbrook High School was established.

Millbrook School, at 430 S. First St., stresses a unique idea in education where the responsibility of attending school rests on the student rather than the school.

Dave Lowe, an educator at the school, feels that if the students are involved in their classes they will attend because they want to learn instead of attending because they're afraid of being dropped from a class.

The non-profit private school is for anyone from kindergarten through 12th grade. There are no grades at Millbrook. The system is essentially pass or fail. Diplomas are presented at the completion of the 210 required credits and are recognized at all colleges.

Students have the opportunity to take classes all year round in subjects like photojournalism, self-defense, violin, yoga, silver-smithing and offset printing.

Members of the school feel the main asset there is the lack of stress and pressure applied to the student. They feel that Millbrook, unlike most public education programs, provides an environment for the student to learn at his own speed.

The school has its drawbacks too, the main one being that it takes a special kind of person to attend. Students who have been conditioned to take orders and follow directions of teachers often cannot adjust to being their own bosses, Lowe said. He added that those who cannot take the responsibility usually return to public schools.

illbrook student Chris Dunkle, right, earns advertising layout from instruct r Mike Rhodes. *3-25-76*

White collars, too

I went to see the movie "Zoot Suit" the other day. It was about how Chicanos in Los Angeles during the 1940s were discriminated against because of the way they dressed.

Wasn't it ironic that I came home to read abut how several Chicanos had been suspended from a local school because "their clothing does not meet the school dress code." Students are being expelled and discriminated against because they do not conform to the white middle class school officials' dress code.

If America is to be truly like a melting pot we must learn to enjoy the spices and flavorings of our various ethnic groups.

Let the students at Hamilton Freshman School dress any way they like. As to the argument that their dress is gang-related — then I say let's expel any student caught wearing a white shirt and is...

Wounding, burning

As the siege of West Beirut continues we hear time and again that Israel is using U.S.-supplied cluster bombs and white phosphorus bombs. Since we're paying for these horrific weapons to be used against the Palestinian and Lebanese people I think it's only fitting that we should know of the damage they do.

Cluster bombs were first used against the people of Vietnam. The variety now being used consists of a cylindrical "mother bomb" which opens in the air and releases 640 bomblets. These round-shaped bomblets each explode, sending shrapnel and as many as 300 pellets into the exposed flesh of anyone around. Cluster bombs are designed for one purpose only; killing and maiming human beings. The pellets are intended to cause ragged, hard-to-heal wounds.

White phosphorus bombs are even more...

'Disgraceful'

After having read the Parade article Sept. 5 "Child on the run" I feel there is an important question to be asked of our society. The article outlines the brutal lives of several of the more than one million runaway children in the United States.

For our government to turn away from these kids and thereby force them into prostitution, drugs and thievery is a telling commentary on its priorities. At a time when we spend hundreds of millions of dollars in military aid to the fascist government of El Salvador we don't have any money to adequately take care of our own youth.

How can this country continue to promote the nuclear arms race, lavishly support dictatorial fascists, and threaten conventional warfare practically everywhere on the planet while at the same time...

Latin
a fir

By BRENDA A
South Valley

Eighteen Latin Ame Committee southeast Fre toward Lem Station wil protesting involvement i

About 60 su

Denied a visa

The Latin American Support Committee and Women's International League for Peace and ... scheduled Dionora

---

MILLBROOK SCHOOL

Course Catalog

March - May 1976

WHERE ARE THEY GOING...?

SCHOOL

TO MILLBROOK SCHOOL!

Lang Russell and Larry Sheehy (after they moved to Ukiah).

This was the first book I wrote, Wild Edibles of Fresno County. David Cox drew some of the illustrations (the cover, for example) and Jim Ashbrook took the photos. I wrote, printed and distributed the book, which was very popular locally. We did three printings and if I have enough time, I might do a fourth printing.

Chapter 6

I helped organize a study group that focused on understanding the broader context of the economic and political systems we live in. I'm not exactly sure when this group came together, but it was probably around 1975. My memory is a little hazy on this, but I think I had approached the Communist Party (CPUSA) and asked them if they could lead the study group. They did not have the capacity to do that, so we formed are own independent group.

We read books and would get together to discuss them once a week. We read Capital Vol 1 by Karl Marx, books about the theory and practice of communism and current books on economic theory from a radical perspective. I liked that we could talk about these issues, ask questions and never feel embarrassed for not knowing all of the answers. This was a very supportive group, which helped me understand the political and economic system we live in.

While all of that was really interesting, the most important thing that came out of those meetings was I met Pam Whalen, who I would marry and have children with. But more about that in a while.

I became (between 1975 and 1976) pretty interested in the Weather Underground and other groups who were taking up arms to overthrow US Imperialism. I was already doing things to support revolutionaries in other countries (like in Angola and Namibia) and was very interested in the idea that perhaps we should be doing more, right here in the belly of the beast, to make it impossible for this country to use its resources to oppress people throughout the world and right here as well. I read a lot about the theory of armed struggle and came close to putting myself into a cell and carrying out armed actions against the state. In the end, I decided that I was not convinced that would be a successful strategy and that there might be other skills that I have that would lead to a better outcome.

This intense reflection on what I was comfortable doing convinced me that I was at a turning point. I could either live a relatively normal life as a middle class American (with progressive politics) or I could decide to dedicate my life to working for social and economic justice. I rejected the extreme position of becoming a soldier in a violent struggle against the state. I simply did not think that was a winning strategy. I opted instead to making revolutionary change a core value of my life, but I was pretty sure I wanted to share my passion with someone and have a family.

After studying Marxism for a couple of years in the study group I was anxious to get out into the world and see things first hand. I was convinced that socialism was a much better economic system than capitalism and really wanted to visit someplace like Cuba so I could see for myself what was going on. Our study group on Marxism (in 1977) meet regularly at Sandra Iyall's house. Sandy had been a friend since the early 70's and she was living with Richard Johnson (who was also in the study group). The other people in the group at the time were Ron Gaul, Kevin Kelly, Teressa (I have forgotten her last name). Teressa and Kevin were Trotskyists which gave us an interesting perspective. Everyone else probably considered themselves independent marxists or socialists. Nobody, other than Kevin and Teressa were in a socialist or communist party.

I'm not sure how it happened, but Ellen Bulf joined the group. She had moved to Fresno from the Bay Area and she was interested in what we were doing. She invited Pam Whalen to the meeting. Pam had been living in Merced and soon moved to Fresno. I remember the first time she came, I was lovestruck. It didn't take long for me to ask her out on a date. First date: Dinner at a Tower District restaurant (Our Town) where we had scallops. In late 1977 some of us in the study group got the idea that we would like to go to Cuba in late December and early January. Pam, Ellen and I planned to go to Mexico City (there was a travel ban in place in the U.S.) to get a Visa to travel to Cuba. Pam and I decided to take the bus and Ellen (who had more money) would fly.

Ellen added this to my Health Blog, which made me very happy. She wrote: "I remember going to a small meeting shortly after you and Pam started going together. We began by going around the room, and when it came to you, you said sort of shyly that you and Pam had been spending time together, which was clearly an understatement... she was sitting opposite you and you looked each other in the eyes and smiled with that glow that spread love all over the room. The expressions on your faces were priceless. Wow–it doesn't seem that long ago but look at the wonderful story which unfolded since then."

By this time I had left Millbrook and was working at a commercial print shop called Creative Teaching Associates. It paid reasonably well (at least compared to what I was had been making) and was a full time permanent job. They were surprised when I said I was going to leave and hoped to come back. They made no promise that the job would be there when I returned (but it was).

In the Sierras reading Prairie Fire, the book published by the Weather Underground about their reasons for using violence in the struggle for social and political change.

Me, Stephanie Malone, Jim Ashbrook and Kim Werner in front of the Upstart Crow bookstore at the Manchester Mall. This photo was taken in late 1977, shortly before Pam and I went to Cuba.

Chapter 7

Pam finished her last day of the semester at CSU-Fresno, we packed and headed to the Greyhound bus depot for our big adventure. I don't really know what Pam was thinking, but I was pretty sure I was in love and wanted to spend the rest of my life with her. The bus ride was, I will say, interesting. I don't remember anyone, speaking English after we left Fresno. Not only did we take the bus, but when we got to Mexico it was the second or third class bus we were on, which meant that it stopped at every little village on the road. OMG, it was a long drive. I was in a bit of culture shock, but Pam (with her fluent Spanish) was just fine.

The tour of Cuba was organized by Anniversary Tours in New York. They were affiliated with the CPUSA and they had full access in Cuba. The most notable things I remember from the trip were:

• On the day before we flew from Mexico City, Pam, Ellen and I went out to eat. Using my best Spanish (ha, ha) I ordered something but ended up getting a very spicy meal I couldn't eat. Ellen helped eat what I had ordered and ended up getting sick. The next morning at the airport, probably because I made her sick, she left her purse in the taxi. Of course, the purse included her money, passport etc. We were in a panic. The flight was about to leave and Ellen could not get on the plane without a passport and Visa. Pam and I gave her all the money we could and she stayed behind, hoping to get an emergency passport at the US Embassy. She did not make it to Cuba.
• On the morning we left Mexico City a woman died of starvation in front of the Catholic Church in the main plaza in downtown (the Zocolo). I was struck by the capitalistic and religious values that would allow a woman to starve to death in front of a church dripping in gold.
• Cuba was amazing. It was clear that it was not a wealthy nation, but it was also obvious that the divide between the rich and poor was minuscule compared to what I had seen in Mexico, the US and Canada.
• The country was set up to benefit poor and working people and to limit the gap between rich and poor.
• That commitment manifested itself in every way imaginable. Everyone had access to health care, public transportation was good and their foreign policy consisted of exporting doctors and teachers.

- When Cuba was involved with foreign military adventures it was to defend and support people who were engaged in struggles for national liberation.
- I realized that they had the ability to teach the truth about the world and their country's history in their schools, unlike what I had experienced in this county. The winners are able to create the narrative by which people develop a world view. The Cubans had museums, schools, books and other ways to educate their citizens about the struggle they were engaged in. The people we spoke with clearly understood the importance of defending the revolution.
- I became convinced that socialism was a realistic and workable system that, given this nation's (the United States of America) wealth and resources, could uplift life for the vast majority of people.
- I fell in love with Pam and looking back on this trip to Mexico and Cuba I think of it as our honeymoon.
- When we arrived back in Mexico Pam and I checked into the Canada Hotel, which was located close to the Zocolo. While there we watched some TV in the hotel. We were seriously impressed with what was going on in Nicaragua. We saw that there was a movement to overthrow the Somoza dictatorship. I saw the trip to Cuba and this moment in time as having a connection and knew then and there that I would become involved with Central America Solidarity work.

Pam and I flew to Puerta Vallarta to vacation for a few days before taking the bus back to Fresno. Back in town we ended up moving in with my friend Richard Gillaspy, who was someone I knew from Millbrook Press. Before long Pam and I rented an apartment on Griffith Avenue (near Blackstone). I easily got my job back at Creative Teaching Associates, which provided enough money to survive. When Pam got pregnant, we moved into a house on Sussex Avenue and that is when Ron Gaul moved in as a roommate.

Politically, Pam and I worked on getting someone from Fresno to attend the World Youth Festival which would be held in Havana in the summer of 1978. We also started the Nicaragua People's Solidarity Committee, which did support work to advance the FSLN in Nicaragua. We openly solicited financial support for the revolutionaries. There was even a group of our friends who decided to go to Nicaragua and fight with the FSLN. Their fundraising efforts included robbing jewelry stores and who knows what else. When at least one of the group was identified at a downtown robbery, he went underground and the other three flew to Costa Rica to integrate into the FSLN on the Southern Front. I raised money from friends to pay for their plane tickets etc.

When the Sandinistas marched into Managua in July of 1979 I felt that the revolutionary forces had momentum and it would not be long before El Salvador, Guatemala and possibly other countries in Central America would win their liberation struggle. We changed the groups name to the Latin American Support Committee and broadened the scope of our work.

We became part of the three national/regional groups doing Central America solidarity work (the Nicaragua Network, CISPES and NISGUA). Pam and I became deeply involved with this work at both the local, regional and national level.

In about September of 1978 we realized that Pam was pregnant. I was, of course thrilled that we were going to have a baby. Pam was pragmatic about the situation and said that we should get married. I loved Pam, but was not convinced that having a piece of paper from the government was a good idea or necessary. She convinced me otherwise. It is not that I did not want to be in the relationship or take responsibility for our child, I just thought all of that could be done outside of a marriage contract. We were married at Betsy Temple's house, by Ellen Bulf (a minister in the Universal Life Church) on October 2, 1979. We got a confidential marriage certificate, which means that it would be really hard for anyone to get the details. Pam says we did that because it was less expensive and that we did not have to get a blood test. That makes sense, because we did not have a lot of money at the time.

In May 1979 our daughter Vanessa was born. This was a huge event in our lives and we made our family life as important as our Central America and other political work. We integrated work (for money), politics and family into who we were. Vanessa came with us to demonstrations, meetings and events. Her first big event was a report back on Guatemala from Billy Monning with the National Lawyers Guild. Monning went on to become a California State Senator. Vanessa was three weeks old at the time.

By the time she was two, Vanessa had probably been to as many demonstrations as some people attend in a life time. I remember her chanting after one of our demonstrations protesting US Intervention in El Salvador. The chant was "No Draft, No War, US Out of El Salvador." Her version of it was "No Giraffes, No War, US Outside the Door." I'm pretty sure, that because our level of activism was so high at that time that Vanessa just assumed that is what everyone does. When she would see cars on the road, she would just assume that everyone was on their way to a meeting, demonstration or other political event. I think it was a little bit of a shock, when she started public school, to realize that ours was an "exceptional" family.

The KKK was active in Fresno, burning crosses, handing out fliers and sometimes holding rallies in town. As a part of our response to their provocative actions, we held an event at the First Christian Church, to counter them. Three or four of us were doing security outside the building to make sure the KKK did not attack us. There had been recent attacks on anti-Klan groups around the country and we wanted to make sure that did not happen to us.

While outside the building I noticed that everything got very quiet all of a sudden. Then, we were surrounded, out numbered and there were bright lights on us. It was the Fresno Police Department. That was the first time I was detained. The police put us in a paddy wagon and interviewed us one at a time.

Some of our security team had brought guns for self protection. With the Marjorie Masson Center (a safe pace for abused women) a couple of doors down, the police had been alerted that there were suspicious guys outside the facility. Once the police realized that we were no threat to the Marjorie Masson Center, they let us go. I was not arrested, but I was impressed with how easily our little security team could be overwhelmed.

Not long after Vanessa was born, I started to organize a union at Creative Teaching Associates. That did not end well. I ended up getting fired and needed to find another job, fast. I decided to take a job at the Fresno Free College Foundation, which is the owner and operator for KFCF 88.1 FM. KFCF is affiliated with Pacifica and rebroadcasts KPFA in Berkeley. Pam and I moved to the Tower District (close to my work) and I enthusiastically started my new job. Most of the work consisted of administrative work (data base management, organizing events etc), but also included some opportunities to produce programing.

I enjoyed working at the station and it wasn't long before I became convinced that there should be more local programing and that we should start recruiting more show hosts to talk about what was going on in Fresno and the Central Valley. Surprisingly, this was not a popular idea with the leadership at KFCF. The primary leadership at the time was Alex Vavoulis, Randy Stover and Rych Withers. Alex was a college professor, Randy was an engineer and most of the stations equipment was at his house and garage. Rych was an engineer. I would be surprised if any of them would identify themselves as political activists and I thought they were not particularly interested in using the station to build a movement for social/political change. They were perfectly happy bringing in the KPFA signal, which was a great service to the community. I thought the station could be that and more.

When I presented my idea of expanding the purpose of KFCF to include more local programing I ran into a wall. I thought that if I could explain my idea to Alex (he was president of the board at the FFCF), he would see the opportunity that existed. I was sadly disappointed that Alex (and the rest of the stations leadership) did not agree with my proposal to bring in more local programing. I suggested to Alex that we do a survey of our members to see what direction they wanted to go in. He said that it would not matter what they wanted, that they were not going to expand local programing.

I tried for a while to organize support to move KFCF in a new direction, but ultimately realized that there were powerful forces that simply did not agree with my opinion. And, those people had the authority to run the station the way they saw fit. Eventually, I had to leave the station because of this political disagreement.

In hindsight, I think it is likely that the FFCF/KFCF board was concerned about political problems that might develop if the station moved in the direction I was suggesting. These kinds of problems had developed in some of the Pacifica stations, which they were aware of, and they did not want to repeat the same mistakes.

Of course, Pam and I were completely consumed with Central America solidarity work at this time, we had a family life and had to make a living. I believe Pam was working at Radio Bilingue at the time. Millbrook Press was coming to the end of its life cycle and they were looking to sell or donate the printing equipment to a local nonprofit.

This was the point in time that I made a decision to leave KFCF and set up a new print shop at Inside/Out, a prison reform group. Inside/Out was publishing prisoner rights manuals and wanted to have their own print shop, so they could print prisoner rights material and bring in some revenue for the nonprofit. I facilitated the transfer of the Millbrook printing equipment to Inside/Out. That pissed off the board of KFCF, because they were also interested in acquiring the presses. Years later, I would find out that several members of the KFCF board of directors accused me of stealing their equipment. It got so bad, that I had to threaten them with a slander lawsuit to get it to stop. The new board president at FFCF apologized for the misinformation and the issue went away, but that experience had an impact on me.

At first, my experience at Inside/Out was good. We set up the shop, printed lots of pamphlets for them and had a successful commercial print shop. I certainly wasn't making a lot of money and Pam and I had some challenging financial times, but we made just enough to survive. I'm not exactly sure of the dates when I worked there, but I think it was somewhere around 1980-83.

In the early 1980's Pam, Vanessa and I moved to a house on Glenn near McKinzie - a nice home in a really challenging neighborhood. We stayed there for a year or so and then bought a house at 1624 E Hedges in the Tower District.

Because of our political activism, life was never dull. I recall one time when we lived on Glenn we had this guy come by, he said he was a neighbor. He told us that he had just got out of prison and he was "down for the revolution." He said that he would do anything and suggested a few things like bank robbery. We told him thank you very much, but we would have to get back to him about that. Of course, we never did. We thought he was probably an undercover cop. We would have people come to our Latin American Support Committee meetings talking about how - that if we were really serious about this work we would be sending guns to the insurgents. They would make these extreme statements and try to provoke the group into taking some kind of illegal actions.

Sometimes we could identify them as government agents and other times we just assumed that they were. One thing I did was to make a FOIA request to the Justice Department to see what files they had on me. At first they wrote back and asked me for more information about what illegal activity I had been up to. Ha, ha. Like someone is going to send them that information. Eventually, they sent a HUGE packet of information showing that they had been following me around from meeting to meeting for a long time. I still have those files.

As time went by at Inside/Out, things became more difficult. Funding was starting to evaporate, the groups CEO Dave Davis became more unstable and eventually things descended into chaos. For me, it started when Dave approached me and asked if I would be willing to print counterfiet money. He said that if I would do that he would stand guard at the door, with a shotgun, and make sure nobody knew what we were doing. I declined. Then, I started noticing a lot of property moving through the facility, which I was pretty sure was stolen. Then, Dave was arrested for illegal weapons sales. It was big news in town and the dynamics at Inside/Out became intense. Dave, who was pretty charismatic (I will give him that), was convinced that the organization was being persecuted and that it was an Us vs. Them situation. There was no middle ground, either you were 100% on board or you were a traitor.

I handed in my resignation because I could not see where all of this was going. I was right. There were a couple of people on the board of directors at Inside/Out that I thought I could talk to about the situation, but it ended up I was wrong. They circled the wagons and anyone who was not onboard with the program was the enemy. When I tried to salvage the printing equipment so it could continue to serve the progressive community in Fresno I was told by one of Dave's associates (a pretty crazy guy who was completely loyal to Dave) that if I persisted I would find myself with a couple of broken legs and who knows what else.

My friend Richard Gillaspy was working at Hume Printing and as I left Inside/Out he helped me get a job at Hume. About two weeks after starting at Hume, I got a call from the Secret Service wanting to know if I could help them with an investigation they were working on. They wanted to know if I knew anything about the printing of money at Inside/Out. Thinking that I did not want to be killed for being a snitch and because I'm generally distrustful of law enforcement I said I knew nothing. About a week later, a story broke in the Fresno Bee about a box of counterfeit money being found at Inside/Out. Shortly after that, Dave Davis ended up dying of a cocaine overdose in his office. Even though the door to his office was locked from the inside, Dave's allies were convinced that he had been murdered by the government. I never thought that, but I was impressed how wrong some of my friends could be. I was probably equally impressed with how people, who you thought were your friends, could so completely betray you.

One person who I thought was a friend even invited me over to his house and tried to get me to implicate myself in some wrongdoing as a way to discredit me. That left me stunned. And, another friend, who we worked closely with in LASC, would absolutely not believe Dave would ever do anything wrong. It was a real eye opening experience to me about the truth, friendship and how you can be ostracized for not going along with a false narrative.

Most of the people at Inside/Out were smart people. I believe that it was a testament to Dave's charisma that people followed him as blindly as they did. There are other examples (way more extreme than this) of intelligent people following a leader they trust to wherever they are taken. The Jim Jones incident in Guyana comes to mind. Don't drink the Kool-aid!

Hume was a big change for me. It was a union print shop, the level of production was massive and it paid well. It was also a really old shop that had some equipment that was unusual. For example, they still set type with a Linotype, which used molten lead. I had never seen a print shop using that kind of technology. I enjoyed working there and before long an opportunity presented itself that would change my life. One of our big customers was The Fresno Bee and when they decided to open an in-plant print shop they asked me to manage it. The pay and benefits were significantly better than what I was currently getting and that had been twice as much as what I earned at Inside/Out or KFCF. I didn't have to think too hard about whether to accept the job or not.

The job as the manager of the in-plant print shop at the Bee changed our lives. We were no longer (barely) living from check to check, but now could think about doing things like. . . taking vacations and not worrying about having enough money to do things like grocery shopping.

While the new job took most of my time, it was not difficult work. I had both the printing and managing skills needed to do the job. If anything, I had to struggle with not getting bored. That was a price I was willing to pay, for the good wages, insurance and descent working conditions.

This was my friend Richard Gillaspy's gift to me when Pam and I got back from Cuba.

Pam and I on a hike in Yosemite shortly before Vanessa was born.

Vanessa liked to ride her dad like a horse. It looks like I was also enjoying spending time with Nessie..

Vanessa and Pam at the end of a march to stop U.S. intervention in Central America.

As busy as we were, Pam and I always took time out to go to Yosemite and other places where we could relax. Of course, that is Vanessa on Pam's lap.

Chapter 8

After a while, it got to be a little challenging to work at such a mainstream job.

In my time off I was working for revolutionary changes. For example, I would take my vacation time to go to Central America where I would spend time doing things like:

- Participating in street demonstrations where we would march with the popular movement in San Salvador (during a civil war) in front of the US Embassy.
- Some of the homes we stayed in had molotov cocktails (a type of gasoline bomb) in the closets.
- We visited war zones.
- One time I took a donation to a Human Rights group in Guatemala that was later (within a week) bombed. Vanessa and I could have easily have been there when it was bombed.
- We spent a significant amount of time in rural Nicaragua while the US backed Contra army had those places under attack.

And, in Fresno we were raising money for the revolution, trying to keep spies and informants out of our group and put pressure on this country to stop intervention in Central America. Pam got arrested at a demonstration at a Congressman's office and the trial that ensued went on for months. I sometimes felt that I lived a double life. During work hours I was known as the pleasant manager of the Fresno Bee's in-plant print shop and in my off hours I was doing things that attracted the attention of the FBI and Justice Department.

Pam and I considered the work we did while in Central America as being so potentially dangerous that we would not travel together. We wanted to make sure that Vanessa would have at least one parent, in case something happened in our travels.

We worked pretty intensely during the 80's on Central America solidarity work. I saved copies of all the fliers, newsletters and news clippings about those days. They are currently in binders in the spare bedroom. I had thought of maybe writing a book about the many interesting things that happened in LASC, but that will only happen if I can live for a few more years.

We also had a family life, doing the things that most families do. We went on vacations (Grand Canyon, hiking in the Sierras, Disneyland etc) One family tradition we started during the 80's was going to Wawona, renting a cabin and staying there for a week in the summer. We must have started in the early 80's because I remember Vanessa being a toddler when we started. Usually, we would rent the cabin with Ellen Bulf, her husband Ira and their daughter Laura.

I liked the trips to Wawona because it was a great place to go, that was close by, and we could just relax. The Merced river was always just down the street and we would go swimming just about every day. I have very pleasant memories of the times spent in Yosemite.

We would also make a summer pilgrimage (each year) to Pam's mom's house in the mountains above Los Gatos. We would go there for Pam's birthday, swim and hike in the nearby Castle Rock Park. Alice (Pam's mom) would usually have a family reunion at her place once a year. Whalen's and Egyed's from far and wide would attend these events. I always felt a little overwhelmed by all of the people, since I was an only child and our family in Fresno was relatively small. I remember we (my family) used to get together for holidays, but there were probably never more than 20 of us. At the Whalen/Egyed family reunions there would be 50 - 100 people.

The other thing I was mindful of at Alice's house, even if there were just the immediate family (Alice, Bob, Mark, Sue and their families) is that people talked really loud. One reason is that most of them (I think Pam is the only one that dodged this bullet) were very hard of hearing. It was a genetic thing that affected just about all of them and their children. So, at times when we were having Thanksgiving or Christmas dinner, it sounded (to me) like everyone was yelling at each other. It was hard for me to get used to how loud it was.

During the 80's and into the 90's Pam and I would drive to The Ranch (Alice's house) for just about every holiday. We would also celebrate the holiday in Fresno to include my mom. Sometimes my mom would go out of town with us, but that didn't happen all that often.

My mom enjoyed spending time with her grandchild, Vanessa. She spent one or two days a week with her and they had a wonderful relationship together. Vanessa was an easy child to raise during that time. She was smart, had lots of friends, a good outlook on life and was just fun to be around. I was always impressed with how trusting she was. She would follow me anywhere. Here is an example of what I'm talking about. When she was maybe 10 years old we ended up in Belize in Central America. We went snorkeling in the coral reefs and spotted a shark. Now, the normal thing to do would be to slowly return to the boat and get the hell out of there. Instead, I motioned to her to follow me as I followed the shark (a nurse shark which I believed was not harmful), which we did. After observing us getting closer and closer, the shark turned toward us and I changed my mind about it being such a good idea to follow the shark. We got back ok, but I was impressed with how Vanessa would follow me anywhere.

Another trip Pam and I took, probably very early in the 1990's, to Guatemala was with Vanessa and her friend Juanita Temple (Betsy's daughter). After hanging out in Antigua for a few days we decided to take our rental car and explore some new parts of the country. We ended up on the road to a national park where, if you were lucky, you would see a Quetzal, the national bird of Guatemala. The route to the Biotopo took us through the highlands, which was the focal point of the civil war at the time. We got lost on the way and it was getting dark. I remember stopping to ask for directions and Pam, who is fluent in Spanish, could not communicate with the person on the side of the road. She only spoke an indigenous dialect. A little while later we picked up a hitchhiker who told us we were not where we thought we were and that we would have to stay in Coban (a small city in the highlands) for the night. The place was so out of the way, they did not have a hotel, but the family who used to run the hotel agreed to put us up for the night. There we were, lost in a small town, in the highlands, with two young girls, during the hight of the civil war. We managed to find our way out of the war zone and ended up at the Biotopo where we stayed in a thatched roof hut and woke up to the sounds of Quetzals in the trees outside.

Pam and I also took a trip in 1986 with about 10 members of the Latin American Support Committee. Before the trip, we raised thousands of dollars and collected a lot of medical supplies. The focus of the trip was to go to Nicaragua and eventually to Somoto, which is a city in Northern

Nicaragua, close to the Honduran border. Because we were well connected, primarily because of Juanita Gomez (Belinda Guerrero's mother), we were treated as honored guests. Juanita knew Daniel Ortega, the president. We were literally brought through the airport as guests of the government, almost like diplomats. A welcome change from the way we were treated in our own country.

This (and that trip to Guatemala) was one of the few times Pam and I travelled together in Central America during the 80's and early 90's), before the end of the civil wars. In Managua we were interviewed at a local radio stations, met with people in the Sandanista Party and eventually headed north to Esteli and Somoto. The trip to Somoto was challenging because there was a war going on and one of the groups we were working with in San Francisco discouraged us from going. Their argument was that it was too dangerous. But, there was more to it than that. They (the S.F. group) had been raising money based on attacks they said were taking place on medical clinics and hospitals near Somoto. They basically ordered us not to go. We, of course, refused. After dropping a lot of our medical supplies off in Esteli we proceeded to Somoto.

When we got to the hospital that we had been told was attacked by the Contras, the director expressed surprise at the story. It became clear that some aspects of the story had been untrue and that the S.F. group was using their false narrative to raise money.

We made our way safely back to Managua and then flew to El Salvador. Our arrival at the El Salvador airport (about 25 miles out of San Salvador) was not as friendly as our Managua experience. Instead of being treated as esteemed guests we were delayed entry after it was discovered that one member of our delegation (Grace Ewert) had a passport that indicated she had visited Eastern Europe. The Cold War was in full effect at the time and the fact that Grace had been to Poland and East Germany was a red flag. Also, I believe one of our other delegation members had literature that might have suggested that we were sympathetic with the Sandinista revolution. The fact that we were flying from Managua was another clue. We were delayed and they told Grace they were going to put her on the next flight out. But, by that time it was getting late and there were no more flights out. We were reluctantly allowed into the country, but by that time it was getting dark. The only road to San Salvador was a known dumping ground for bodies by the military and death squads. There was only one or two taxi drivers still at the airport, so we thought ourselves lucky to get one of them to agree to drive us to town at a reasonable rate.

Once in the car and driving down that dark and isolated road (appropriately enough there was lots of lightening and thunder at the time) the taxi driver informed us that there were often robberies along the road, he said carried out by the FMLN (the revolutionary forces in El Salvador). If that happened (a barricade and attempted robbery) he would not stop. He said it was his plan to drive through the barricade and that we should all get down on the floorboard to make it less likely that we would be shot and killed. I thought we were all going to die. We told him that if he would stop, we would be fine with giving money to the FMLN. He refused. By the time we got to the end of the road, without an incident, we were stopped by the military. They asked the taxi driver what things were like on the road, presumably because they knew how dangerous it was and didn't want to check it out themselves.

One of the memorable visits we made in San Salvador was at a Human Rights office. The person leading the discussion was available because she had not been around the previous week when the military arrested all of the workers at the center. She said that she fully expected them to come back and arrest her, take her to jail, where she would be tortured and probably killed (maybe being dumped on the road to the airport). She went over the human rights situation in the country, documented the abuses and encouraged us to get the word out about what was going on.

One of our delegation members became increasingly upset about the situation and insisted that if we were serious then we needed to basically sell everything we owned and support groups like the Human Rights center. He felt that if they would risk their lives, the least we could do would be to provide them with the resources we had available. This suggestion did not sit well with everyone else and there became a split in our group. The people taking that position decided to set up a material aid project They were really very dedicated to that mission, but we ended up not working very closely together, because of the hostility that had developed.

Over time, hurt feelings healed and we were able to work together, but never as closely as before. After El Salvador most of the delegation flew back to Fresno. Grace Ewert and I flew to Belize for a few days. Belize was different from the other countries in Central America we had visited and it was hard at first to wrap our minds around why that was the case. I remember us being impressed with how many people would "befriend" us as we simply walked down the street. They wanted to be your tour guide, show you around town (Belize City) or get you to one of the islands. Grace and I wondered around for a day or two just trying to figure out what was going on, since it was so different from Nicaragua and El Salvador. We ended up on a small island where we went snorkeling and just relaxed. It was absolutely gorgeous, off the beaten path and not at all expensive.

It has occurred to me that my traveling to Belize with another woman might be seen as something I should not have done. But, I think it reflects on how much Pam and I trusted one another. Nothing inappropriate happened on the trip to Belize with Grace and jealousy was never an issue in our marriage.

The next year (1987) Pam and I decided we needed more space and thought about adding a bedroom and bathroom to our Hedges house, but it would have been too expensive. While we were, more or less, happy with the neighborhood we expanded our search for a new house to include the Fresno High and Old Fig Garden areas. Pam and I found a house on Lansing Way (near Palm), but it was too expensive. We could have only afforded it if we restricted our diet to rice and beans and walked to work.

Eventually, in April or May, we found our house at 4773 N Arthur Ave. It had almost everything we wanted and was priced right, being West of Palm in what most people would consider a less desirable neighborhood than Old Fig. But, it was perfect for us. Three bedrooms, two baths and a pool. Yahoo!

Vanessa was sad to leave the Hedges house and for a while stayed in touch with at least one of the kids from the old neighborhood (Claudia). We had some neighbors with kids her age at the new house and she soon found out how much fun a pool could be for kids. Not a big surprise. Saul and Patrick and their cousins were soon regular visitors at our house. Vanessa joined the Girl Scouts about that time, which brought in even more visitors to our pool.

In August of 1989 Simone was born. I remember Pam telling me she was pregnant (we were at Wawona at the time) and I was so happy, but surprised. I had been planing to take some time off from work at the Fresno Bee, go to Central America with Vanessa and study Spanish. Having a baby on the way made me rethink those plans. I decided to still take some time off, but not as long as I had originally planned. Vanessa and I flew to Guatemala in early 1989 and went to Antigua where we enrolled in Spanish language classes. It was really difficult for me to pick up the language, but we kept at it for a couple of weeks. Antigua is just a great place to be. The weather is almost always great, there are lots of language schools and enough infrastructure to make you feel comfortable. Vanessa was 10 at that time. It was on this trip that when I realized for the first time, Vanessa was becoming an adolescent.

Before then, she would cheerfully do whatever I asked her to do. Like I said earlier, she would follow me anywhere. She was different in Antigua and I had a hard time figuring out what was going on. I'm not sure if she even knew what was going on. What I noticed was that Vanessa was more willful and not interested in my suggestions. I didn't really know what was going on, but I could tell something had changed.

Still, we had a good time in Guatemala, learning Spanish, hanging out together and getting to know some of the people and places. I recall we took a two day trip with a very informal guide. The guide was German, spoke English and there were 5 or 6 of us that loaded into his van for a trip to more rural parts of the country.

We stayed in a very small village where we stopped before going on to some caves. There was a restaurant we stopped at (open air with a few tables and chairs under some palm fronds). When we selected chicken from the extremely limited menu, the person taking the order told a couple of young boys to go catch the chickens. Which they did - you could see the dust and feathers flying.

We drove to this amazing cave where a river was flowing out of a hole in the side of a mountain. Next to that were the caves. Inside the caves they had a 40 watt bulb every 30 feet or so. To move through the cave, you had to walk over ladders that were put across bottomless pits. It was insane. I'm sure that if Pam was there she would have wacked me on the side of the head for even considering entering such a place. Somehow we survived. We were told upon leaving that at dusk you can stand at the entrance to the cave with your flashlight and watch the bats (tens of thousands of them) fly out and around you. We were assured that the bats would not hit you. Our group did not test that theory. Instead, we headed back to the village for dinner.

Our lodging was a mud and stick structure with a straw roof and cardboard for the interior walls. The light was a single bulb situated between two rooms in a cutout in the cardboard. I remember being warned to shake out my shoes in the morning to make sure there were no scorpions inside. The tour concluded with a trip to the biotopo to look for Quetzals. We were stopped along the way at a military checkpoint (keep in mind that this was in the middle of the civil war) and they sprayed the van for pests with some white powder (DDT?). I'm sure that was not good for our health. All in all, that was a very interesting side trip.

Before returning home, Vanessa and I flew to Jamaica. Why we ended up going there I don't recall. It just seemed like a good idea at the time. For whatever reason, the flight to Jamaica and back to Fresno mysteriously never showed up on my credit card bill. So, it was a great trip and the price was right. We arrived in Montego Bay, rented a car and drove to Negril. On the drive out of the airport I was distracted by marijuana vendors openly selling their product from a round about. The drive down the coast was beautiful, the beaches were great and Vanessa and I had a good time before flying back to Fresno.

Pam and Vanessa on one of our many trips to the Sierra mountains.

Alice Whalen, Pam and Vanessa at our new home, which we bought at 1624 E Hedges Avenue in Fresno.

My mom Vie and her first grandchild, Vanessa. They spent a lot of time together.

From left to right: Randy Dotta, Steve Bruin, Grace Ewert, Juanita Gomez, Patrick Young, Junko Kunitake, Mike Rhodes and Pam Whalen just before the 1986 trip to Central America.

The LASC delegation at the hospital in Somoto where we delivered $7,000 in material and financial aid.

This demonstration LASC organized in front of the Federal Building in downtown
Fresno in October 1986 was one of many we held during that time. That is Junko
Kunitake being photographed by a government photographer.

Junko Kunitake and Patrick Young drove buses to El Salvador and Nicaragua
delivering material aid to communities in those countries.

LATIN AMERICAN SUPPORT COMMITTEE
P.O. Box 4496
Fresno, California 93744

NEWSLETTER

FEBRUARY 1986

Meeting Every Tuesday 7:00 PM
Ted Wills Community Center

Fresno 11 Put War on Trial

The trial of the Fresno 11 which riveted community attention for two weeks finally ended in a hung jury on Feb 10. The 11 LASC members had been arrested when they were protesting the U.S.-supported bombing of civilians in El Salvador at Congressperson "Chip" Pashayan's Fresno office on Sept. 25, 1985. They hoped to use the proceedngs "to put the war on trial."

The fact that the District Attorney was unable to get a conviction for tresspassing from 12 impartial jurors underscores the support that exists in Fresno for peace activists' right to protest the role of the U.S. in this illegal and immoral war. In spite of the fact that the defendants, who represented themselves, were not allowed to talk about the reasons for their action and events in

CONTINUED ON PAGE 4

SC████████)

EL SALVADOR WORK
NICARAGUA FUND RAISING
Treasurer
Newsletter Editor
Literature
Membership
Emergency Response

(u)

Also identified in the newsletter, apparently
as its official photographer is ████████████ (u)

A correspondent for the newsletter is identified
as ████████ (further identified in the newsletter
as a Counselling Professor at CALIFORNIA STATE UNIVERSITY,
FRESNO (CSUF).\(u)

The following eleven individuals ████████
████████████████████ were arrested in September,
1985, as a result of a sit-in at the offices of representative
CHARLES PASHAYAN, in Fresno. The protestors, all
believed to be members of the LASC, were opposed to
PASHAYAN's support of the Government of El Salvador.
The eleven were identified as follows:\(u)

(u)

(u)

(u)

This was the office in Guatemala City where Vanessa and I visited, shortly before it was bombed.

Vanessa and I at the Biotopo in Guatemala where we did see the Quetzal.

Vanessa and I went to Antigua, Guatemala in 1989.

These photos were taken shortly after we bought our new house at 4773 N Arthur Ave.

Vanessa and her friend Claudia at Fresno City College.

This group of LASC members crated and shipped this printing press to El Salvador.

Chapter 9

I returned to work at The Fresno Bee, life returned to normal and before long Simone was born. I have to admit that the thought of starting all over again with a newborn was a little daunting and I wondered if maybe we were a bit crazy (and old) to be going down this road. I thought that if we had decided not to have a second child that before long, Vanessa would be grown up and our responsibilities would not be as great and we might have to work less and could play more.

A year or so after Simone was born I even had somewhat of a mid-life crisis. In my mind I was feeling a little overwhelmed with responsibility and thought - is this it? Is this all there is going to be in my life? I know, now it seems like an immature thought and it probably was. But, I just couldn't get past the fact that I was totally and irrevocably tied down. I had no choice but to work at a job that I was bored with. Plus, the job took a lot of my time. After work all of my time was taken up with either childcare, mundane household chores or political work (mostly Central America solidarity work at that time). It took a while, but I came to the realization that I was living the life that I had set up and things were going pretty well. It was that change of perspective that got me over that hump.

Pam and I lived pretty much from paycheck to paycheck until around this time, but at some point with us both working at jobs that paid well we were able to get a little ahead. When that happened, it was like a weight being lifted off my shoulders. Over the next ten or fifteen years we would get to the point to where we had all of the money we needed to cover our expenses and we did not have to worry about unexpected expenses. Today, money is just something we use to pay for what we need to survive, help our kids (with things like getting into a home they own) and to provide for my mom in her old age. It is great not worrying about money and my future. It should be like this for everyone.

Our family took a memorable trip to Mexico when Simone was just a few months old (late 1989). We drove the entire length of Baja in a van. We stopped in Guerrero Negro where the whales go to have their babies and got to La Paz where we took a ferry to the mainland. The most exciting thing that happened is that we left our baby carriage on a cliff overlooking a beach, along with Pam's purse which contained some of our money and credit cards.

That delayed our catching the ferry to the mainland. While stuck in La Paz I convinced Pam that we should check with the police to see if anyone turned in the baby carriage. To our great surprise we were told that there was a radio announcement about the incident. Someone who was an announcer at a radio station spotted the baby carriage, thought that a distraught mother might have taken the baby and jumped off the cliff and into the ocean. When we showed up at the radio station to claim the purse and baby carriage it was big news. Pam was interviewed on radio and TV about this man bites dog story. Usually, the story is that some tourist was robbed while in Mexico. This was a story that reversed the standard narrative - the Gringo tourist was helped (not harmed) by a good samaritan.

The early 1990's was a time when I had shifted my political work from working locally to where I was the Regional Coordinator of the Nicaragua Network. That work meant flying to Washington DC every six months or so and having more interaction with Nicaragua oriented groups on the West Coast. It was a big responsibility and it meant working with a lot of groups that did not always see things the same way. I was able to build unity between groups that had a long history of not getting along, started a regional newsletter so all of the groups knew what was going on and held conferences and regional meetings.

I also created an Emergency Response Network that had the capacity to respond when there were human rights violations in Central America. It was a membership organization - the members would pay for us to send Telex's, Faxes, or pay for newspaper ads when a union leader or political activist was jailed or killed. The project was very successful and was often able to create enough publicity to force the government (in a country like El Salvador, Guatemala or Honduras) to acknowledge that somebody was in custody and that people around the world were watching. I'm sure it saved lives and I was excited to be a part of the project. It also took a lot of time and between working at The Fresno Bee, being the West Coast Regional Coordinator for the Nicaragua Network, doing local solidarity work and having a family life, I was busy all of the time.

Not surprisingly, family life took more of my attention, given we had a baby and Vanessa was starting to enter puberty. I ended up taking a one year leave at work while I focused on the home front and continued with my other activities. I found that time rather challenging because there was no obvious path to success when my daughter started to become her own person.

Neither Pam or I was prepared for what in retrospect was a rather routine transition from a young child to a teenager. As much as I would like to take credit for her remarkable transformation into the great person she has become, I give credit where it is due - Vanessa found her way through those challenging times and has lived a remarkable life - getting a great education, traveling around the world (several times) and she is now married and starting a family. I'm extremely proud of her, but it sure would have been good to have had a crystal ball back in those days.

Not knowing how things are going to end up is what makes life interesting. You do the best you can to set up a good outcome and in the end there are so many factors in play that you don't know what the outcome will be. I feel like that with my cancer diagnosis - at this point all I can do is go down the path of treatment (immunotherapy, radiation, changes in diet etc) and hope for the best. Life gives you no guarantees about how things will turn out. You have control of those factors that you are able to manipulate, but there are so many other things in play that will determine the outcome that it seems like your fate is in the hands of a cosmic game of dice.

I have lived a reasonably healthy life. I ate well, exercised never smoked and yet I end up with 4th stage lung cancer. How is that fair? Now, all I can do is go down a path of treatment that will, hopefully, give me a few more years to live. Life is not fair, but there is nothing to be gained by bemoaning your fate. It is what it is. I'm just glad that I can look back on my life and feel satisfied with the things I have done. If I get more time, great. If I loose the next roll of the dice, then I will go knowing that I did the best I could and I will appreciate having this time to reflect back on my life.

During the early 1990's our solidarity work led us to form a sister city with Telpaneca in Nicaragua. We did a lot of things with this sister city project, but a couple of things that stand out are:

• We built a school for them.

- We were able to bring a number of folks from Telpaneca to Fresno to help people understand what was going on there.
- There were several delegations of visitors from Fresno that went to Telpaneca.
- We raised thousands of dollars for a scholarship project that allowed many students to continue with their education.

This was Simone's first step. She was exactly one year old. She is walking from Pam to her big sister Vanessa.

Kaila Igasan and Simone. They were and still are good friends.

Simone, Sylvia Flores (a good friend of Vanessa's), Patrick Esquivel , and Vanessa in our living room.

Simone was a happy child who grew up in a secure and loving family.

Mike, Simone, Vanessa and Pam at Castle Rock Ranch where Pam's family grew and sold Christmas trees.

This is the school we built in Telpaneca, Nicaragua.

Chapter 10

Towards the end of the 90's my focus began to shift from Central America. There was an interesting development in the organized labor movement that got my attention. The national AFL/CIO announced that they were going to make needed changes in their policies. Those changes would direct locals to organize the unorganized, work with Labor/Community Alliances and to see immigrants as allies (as opposed to calling for their deportation).

Joining with a local group that emerged in 1996 Pam and I helped found the Frank Little Chapter of the Labor Party. The Labor Party was a national group, based in organized labor, that felt a third party was needed because the bosses already had two (the Republicans and Democrats). It was an idea that, I believe, the AFL/CIO was using nationally to put pressure on the Democrats to be more sympathetic to organized labor.

Frank Little was a member of the Industrial Workers of the World and he was active in Fresno. Little was involved in the 1910/11 Free Speech fight, where workers fought for and won the right to organize. The Fresno police were arresting them for standing up on a box and talking about the union. As soon as one organizer was arrested another one would take their place. The IWW sent so many people to Fresno to organize that the jails were filled up. When word came that there was a train on its way to Fresno filled with IWW organizers, the city backed down and agreed that they would allow people to talk about the union on the streets of Fresno. The IWW won that Free Speech fight.

The Frank Little chapter of the Labor Party held meetings at the Fresno Center for Nonviolence and soon decided to establish a publication to educate and mobilize this new (Labor/Community) alliance. Of course, the result was the birth of the Labor/Community Alliance newsletter. This story, which is a big part of my life, has many twists and turns. I produced a video, which tells some of that history. You might want to take a look at that video here: https://www.youtube.com/watch?v=0tXK7no90VU

The newsletter, which started out being printed on copy machines at union locals, was always viewed as an organizing tool. We wanted to educate both union and community members about the struggles that were taking place in Fresno and build unity. There was nothing else like the Labor/

Community Alliance. There were lots of individual newsletters that focused on single issues - like the Sierra Club or WILPF newsletter. The L/CA was different because we included information from a wide variety of unions and community groups and distributed it much more broadly than any other group could have done. The Peace and Social Justice Calendar was an important part of the paper - because now we could start to coordinate events, not planning too many things for one day.

A big decision for me happened just after we started the Labor/Community Alliance. I had not been happy at The Fresno Bee for years, but felt like I was trapped, even though I knew I had the key to my freedom. The job paid really well, had great benefits and I could do the work in my sleep. How could any sane person voluntarily leave all of that behind?

It was a hard decision to make and I was stressed about how things would go.   It was like jumping off a cliff without knowing what was on the other side. The one thing that made it even possible to consider such a move was that Pam had a good job at SEIU, which would provide us with one good salary and enough insurance coverage that we wouldn't have to go through bankruptcy if one of us got sick.

When I was getting ready to leave it occurred to me that since I knew so many people at The Bee and that a lot of them were being under-paid, did not have great benefits and they had no grievance procedure that they might want to join me in organizing a union.

Since I had lots of personal contacts at The Bee, I pitched the idea to a couple of unions and was hired as a "lost timer" to start organizing. A lost timer is paid the salary they had been making while organizing for the union.

It was a brutal campaign. I really had no idea what I was getting into. The Bee is incredibly anti-union and would stop at nothing in their effort to defeat our organizing effort. They put my mug shot on a flier and told all security to keep me off the property. They brought in a team of union busters to advise them what else to do.

I was surprised to hear that they held captive meetings with employees (in other words, workers had to attend their propaganda sessions) where they were told that their jobs would be outsourced if they voted for the union. That was in the Advertising Art department. In the Transportation department they were told that there would be mandatory drug tests if they voted for the union. Transportation drivers worked late at night and the fact is that some of them smoked pot as they delivered papers to the carriers. Management told them that if they voted for the union, they would implement drug tests. If they voted against the union they would not have to worry about it. They would bring in workers for one on one meetings to threaten and intimidate them based on the particular workers individual issues. If they smoked pot, they would threaten them with drug tests. If they had reliability issues (being late to work, for example) they were told that could be overlooked, but if they supported the union, they would be fired. Our lead organizer in transportation was fired on bogus charges. It went on and on. Most of the workers got really scared and we lost the election.

I had a nightmare during that time. I was flying a large plane with lots of passengers and I realized that I had no idea how to fly that thing and that we were all going to crash and burn. I wonder where that dream came from? Even with all of the help I got from Pam, other organizers and many workers who were pro union, we just did not have access to talk to the workers enough or to convince them that the union would increase their wages and defend them against management attacks. That was a real lesson to me. Organizing, particularly in the private sector, is really hard.

Of course we filed complaints with the National Labor Relations Board, because The Bee violated the law on so many levels, but after the election it really didn't matter. The amount they had to pay to the workers who filed complaints was chump change compared to what it would have cost them if we had won the election. The Bee was a business that would do whatever it takes to win, including breaking the law.

After The Bee I continued working as a union organizer at CSU-Fresno working for the California Faculty Association. I enjoyed that work. It was much calmer than The Bee organizing campaign. All I really had to do was to meet with new faculty members, tell them about the union and sign them up. No threats or intimidation. Faculty were able to make a decision whether or not they wanted to join the union free from coercion, threats and intimidation.

Vanessa and Simone at the Martin Luther King march in 2001. I don't think that it happened that year, but at an MLK march I lost Simone and her friend Kayla. I was supposed to be watching them, but we got separated when buses drove everyone to CSUF to hear a speech by one of MLK's children. Simone and Kayla's bus did not go to CSUF, but rather to a parking lot downtown. OMG! It turned out they were fine, but I was in some serious trouble with Pam when she found out.

Simone and Pam on a trip we took to Hungary and Romania. Actually, Simone and I had also visited England with my mom on that trip, but Vie flew back and did not come with us to Hungary. Also on the trip was Pam's mom and Frances, who I believe is one of Pam's cousins. This photo was taken in a tower in Hungary.

Simone and my mom in Trafalgar Square playing with the pigeons.

Labor/Community ALLIANCE

VOLUME 3, ISSUE 7   609   AUGUST 1998

Workers organize at The Fresno Bee
News you won't find in The Bee
by Brian McNally

On July 13, just ten days away from their union election date, the pressroom employees of *The Fresno Bee* congregated at a local Denny's restaurant to hold what they hoped would be one of their last meetings without union representation in the workplace. It was last fall, several years after *The Fresno Bee* had successfully chased the unions out, that workers from the pressroom and the packaging and distribution departments decided they were fed up with the poor treatment they were receiving from management and sought to regain union affiliation.

As the election date approached, the company began asking for six more months to prove that they would respond to their employees' grievances. But the workers recognized this request as an attempt to trick them. Management wanted to derail their organizing efforts with promises that might be delivered for six months if they were lucky, but most likely would be discarded the day after the election. Allen Washington, a *Bee* pressroom employee, exclaimed in reaction to the company's ruse, "We don't need to give the company six months. We gave them five years."

Those five years after the pressroom employees lost their union representation—and the ten years from the time packaging and distribution employees lost theirs—began

Photo by George Elfie Ballis

with fulfilled promises from management at *The Fresno Bee*. The company had given the workers its word that it would treat them better if they decertified their unions. But it wasn't long before the company began to abuse its power over the recently un-unionized workers. First management began to reduce the number of employees on each shift. Then retired workers weren't being replaced. And when employees called in sick, their shifts weren't being covered. In the printroom, this reduction in the number of workers assigned to a given shift was causing safety hazards.

The company also began to use its apprenticeship program in the pressroom as a source of cheap labor rather than a skills-building system. In packaging and distribution, good-paying full-time jobs were turned into part-time positions that offered little more than the minimum wage. The list of abuses kept mounting: safety compromises, favoritism in the

(continued on p. 6)

Inside This Issue

Letters to the Editor 2
California Politics 3
Pastors for Peace Head for Cuba 4
August Labor/Community Events 5
Stand Up for Human Rights 7

Labor Day Picnic
Sunday, Sept. 6 • Noon - 6 p.m.
California State University, Fresno
CENTRAL LABOR COUNCIL

FIRST PRINCIPLE: UNITY

Fresno Bee fires employee for union organizing

by Mike Rhodes, Labor/Community Alliance

 On Wednesday, September 2, *The Fresno Bee* fired Jerald Haydostian because he was actively organizing a union in the transportation department. Haydostian has worked as a driver at *The Fresno Bee* for 17 years. The Communications Workers of America immediately filed an unfair labor practice with the National Labor Relations Board (NLRB). Now, we are asking for your support in this labor dispute.

Workers in the transportation department filed a petition for an election with the NLRB on the very day Haydostian was fired. Some of us don't believe his termination was a coincidence. Jerry started the organizing drive in the transportation department. Without him, the effort to build a union would not have gotten off the ground. Through Haydostian's efforts an organizing committee was formed and an overwhelming majority of co-workers signed union authorization cards.

The Bee alleges that on August 26 Haydostian lied to his supervisor when he requested time off to help his sick mother; she was admitted to Saint Agnes Medical Center the next day. The bogus charge that Haydostian was fired for lying is nothing more than an excuse to cover *The Bee's* real motivation, which is to stop the union organizing drive in the transportation department.

We demand a public apology from *The Fresno Bee* for this outrageous and illegal act to destroy the union. We further demand *The Fresno Bee* immediately reinstate Haydostian and give him full back pay. We are calling on our friends in the Labor/Community Alliance to support us in this struggle by contacting publisher Keith Moyer and letting him know what you think about *The Fresno Bee's* treatment of its workers. For more information, contact:

Transportation Department Organizing Committee
Communications Workers of America Local 9408
130 W. Shields, Fresno CA 93705
248-9408   clr2@igc.apc.org

The Fresno Bee will be forced by the National Labor Relations Board to reinstate Jerald Haydostian and give him full back pay because he was, without a doubt, fired illegally. *The Bee* wants this process to take as long as possible. *The Bee* would like to wait until after the election for union representation before it brings Jerry back. Why?

❶ As long as Jerry is not in the transportation department, he can't talk with his co-workers about the union.

❷ His firing is a form of intimidation.

❸ They want transportation department employees to think that they will be fired if they visibly support the union.

Our best hope for getting Jerry back on the job right away is to turn up the heat on *The Fresno Bee*. *The Bee* has to know that people in Fresno care about this issue. That means that YOU have to call or write Keith Moyer, the publisher, and tell him what you think about this outrageous firing. We can't let them get away with this!

Contact Keith Moyer at *The Fresno Bee* about this incident at 441-6060; The Fresno Bee, 1626 E Street, Fresno CA 93786; or kmoyer@fresnobee.com.

Labor Day Speech

by Jerald Haydostian

(Given at the Labor Day Picnic sponsored by the Fresno/Madera/Kings/Tulare Central Labor Council, Building Trades Council & Coalition of Labor in Fresno.)

Before last week I would have avoided public speaking like the plague because I am so shy. But there is an incredible purpose behind all this that goes beyond my personal limits. I was asked to speak today because I am a perfect example of a worker willing to risk everything just to make conditions better for my fellow employees.

The Fresno Bee took me up on that offer by taking everything away, firing me for organizing our department and using me as an example to instill fear in others to discourage anyone else from continuing my efforts. For reasons like this, we have, and will exercise, the right to stand up to companies like The Fresno Bee that seem to think they can get away without providing the necessities of life for people who break their backs to make them record profits.

(continued on p. 6)

Why are workers organizing at *The Bee*?

Workers in the transportation department at *The Fresno Bee* are organizing a union because:

➲ They are given no dental or health care benefits.

➲ Transportation drivers are forced to work all holidays and receive no extra pay for working those days.

➲ They have no sick leave.

➲ Employees in transportation get no paid vacation time.

➲ They work up to 35 hours a week but are classified as part-time employees to avoid paying benefits.

➲ Drivers earn little more than minimum wage. Someone with 15 years' experience might make $10 an hour.

➲ They want an end to favoritism by supervisors and managers.

Chapter 11

In May 2000 nineteen activists got arrested at Fashion Fair for protesting The Gap's use of sweatshop labor. I was one of them - the first time I had ever been arrested. We fought the charges and ended up suing the owner of Fashion Fair and getting a sizable settlement. We also learned that the police had sent an informant into our group. We learned about that in discovery - but I knew that something was up when I would get calls from the police asking about this or that protest that we were talking about having. It was like, how do they know that information when we weren't even sure ourselves if we were going to have a protest at that place and at that time? It was weird.

Following our victory, Fashion Fair continued to block people from handing out fliers at the mall, threatening them with arrest. So, I organized a July 4 reading of the Constitution and the Bill of Rights at the front door of Fashion Fair. They, of course, threatened us with arrest up until the last second, but they did not arrest us. I could just imagine the publicity - group arrested for reading the Constitution on the 4th of July. I don't think Fashion Fair wanted that kind of publicity. But, we learned some valuable lessons about Free Speech.

I always liked this quote by Utah Phillips about Free Speech:

"The state can't give you free speech, and the state can't take it away. You're born with it, like your eyes, like your ears. Freedom is something you assume, then you wait for someone to try to take it away. The degree to which you resist is the degree to which you are free..."

We used the Utah Phillips quote a lot to remind people about what was at stake in defending our Free Speech rights. Utah Phillips came to Fresno a number of times and even stayed one night at our house.

The Labor/Community Alliance continued to grow and expand. In 2002 I started writing about the homeless. That could be a story in and of itself. Well, I did write a book about it, so there is a lot to tell. Rather than try to repeat that story here, I will refer you to my book, Dispatches from the War Zone, which is available at local bookstores and on Amazon.

Publishing the book got the American Civil Liberties Union of Northern California to organize a book tour in 2016 where I was able to speak, sell books and which allowed them to organize around the homeless issue with their chapters throughout Northern California. Pam and I went to Eureka/Arcata, Redding, Chico, Monterrey and Santa Cruz. I also, independently of the ACLU, did numerous book readings in Fresno, Merced and other places.

While the homeless issue was something we regularly wrote about in the L/CA there were lots of other issues worthy of coverage.

We had an article early on about how sheepherders were being exploited. Not only did the article win an award from New American Media, but legislation was passed in Sacramento providing protection to sheepherders, in part, due to our efforts to expose the injustices.

There was a fantastic article that Mark Arax and his students wrote about the horrific conditions in the Fresno County Jail, where inmates were being denied medications that were needed to maintain their mental health. That investigation led to the changing of policy and the saving of lives.

Three books have been written based on the stories in the Community Alliance. My book, Richard Stones book "Hidden in Plain Sight" and Boston Woodard's "Inside the Broken California Prison System."

An important project that I organized in 2004 was the Central Valley Progressive PAC. It seemed to me that if people on the left could unite and have a strategic plan for electoral politics we could win political power in Fresno. I made the proposal, brought people together who were interested in the idea and formed the organization. I thought it was so obvious that if we formed this organization to win political power, it would not take long before we achieved our goal. As with many good ideas, it is much harder to implement than to think up. And, since I was pretty busy with other projects (being the editor of the Community Alliance newspaper, working on the homeless issue, etc) it wasn't the only thing I was doing.

When you are talking about something as important as winning political power, there are so many ways things can go wrong. There are divisions about whether to support Democrats or Third Party candidates. Even if you were just working with the Democrats you would be dealing with progressive vs. corporate (Blue Dog) Democrats. Do you support someone because they have the most progressive politics (even if they don't have a snow balls chance in hell of winning) or do you support someone who is more moderate and can run a viable campaign that would defeat a knuckle dragging Republican? Or, do you push for the most progressive candidate who would loose, giving us a Republican Congressperson?

I continue to believe that the CVPPAC can be a significant factor in winning local political power and I will work on this project to the end. But, I'm impressed with how difficult it is to build unity on the left around electoral politics. Funny, it seems like I should have known that would be the case. Maybe I'm not as clever as I think I am. Or, maybe I'm just pathologically optimistic.

One project that resulted in our ability to illustrate voting patterns in the City of Fresno was a map I designed and printed in the Community Alliance. The map shows a pattern of high voter turnout in the more affluent parts of the city (north) and how those votes are overwhelmingly conservative. The opposite is true in southeast and southwest Fresno where low voter turnout is common, but they consistently vote for more progressive candidates and issues. It is my perspective that Fresno and the Central Valley are not as conservative as people say. We just don't have a level playing field where poor and working people can vote as easily as the affluent.

Pam and I have had two radio shows on KFCF. Street Heat started in March 1998 and was connected with the Labor/Community Alliance. Stir it Up was set up several years later after a huge conflict at the radio station, in which there was an effort to remove the existing board of directors and replace it with a group that wanted more local programing. The overthrow failed and within a couple of weeks, the station offered several community groups their own show. Pam and I accepted the time slot on behalf of the newspaper. Program slots were also given to the Green Party, the Fresno Center for Nonviolence and Women's International League for Peace and Freedom.

I was a co-founder and on the board of the Community Media Access Collaborative (CMAC) and was one of a few people that pushed for that to become a reality. CMAC now has a studio, equipment and training for community members to produce video and get it seen on Comcast cable.

This was one of those projects where the money from Comcast was just sitting there and all we really had to do is ask for it. Well, it was more complicated than that, but having a community access channel, the studio, equipment and staff is a really big deal. A lot of people I know have gone through the training and have produced shows. I consider that a victory that will have a long term impact in this community.

I established a Central Valley page on Indymedia, which is an Internet based self-publishing website. That is significant because Indymedia is a platform that anybody can directly publish on. If you have an article, audio or video about events that are important, you can publish them on Indymedia. The project emerged during the anti-globalization (WTO) demonstrations in Seattle, which happened in 1999. Indymedia gave people a way to distribute information outside of the mainstream media. It took a few years for the idea to take root in the Central Valley, but I was one of the people who made that happen.

In 2006 I was invited by Fresno Magazine to write a column for their monthly magazine. I was the "LEFT" side of a right/left dialog. Each month me and the guy representing the right would have space to write about an important issue. Reproductive rights, the war in Iraq and the death penalty are the sorts of issues we would write about. They paid me and I was able to reach a whole new audience so it worked for me. Plus, it was always a challenge to make a coherent argument about a topic of great importance, using a limited number of words (I think it was something like 750 words). The writing assignment lasted about 5 years.

This is the moment I got arrested at Fashion Fair mall for protesting The Gaps use of sweatshop labor.

This was our July 4th event at Fashion Fair mall where we read the Constitution and Bill of Rights. They threatened us with arrest, but in the end we prevailed and made our point - that Free Speech is only a reality if you stand up for your right to use it.

The one and only Utah Phillips.

Pam and Utah Phillips at the KFCF studio.

Frank Little

Frank Little

Protecting our Resources

Who best represents the interests of the environment?

Progressives, those of us on the Left of the political spectrum, best represent the interests of the environment because we believe that humans are a part of nature, and that in order to survive we must balance our use of the natural resources with the needs of the planet. Contrast this philosophy with those on the Right, who believe man was put here to dominate and control nature for his own ends. In their worldview, it is all about exploiting the environment for their own enrichment. You can decide for yourself which of these two philosophies represents the best interests of the environment.

The policies of the Right have led to the environmental disasters that most of us are familiar with -- global warming, air pollution, water pollution, and the destruction of entire species of plants and animals in the

> "The Left has fought tirelessly to strengthen regulations on corporations and individuals that defile our environment..."

world. If we continue down this path, we will find ourselves in a world that is so far out of balance, that life as we know it will cease to exist.

The Left has fought tirelessly to strengthen regulations on corporations and individuals that defile our environment while the right has beat the drum for deregulation and weakened government oversight. The Right would love nothing more than to

and newspapers. Many environmentalists have bought hybrid cars and will be the first to buy all electric vehicles when they are available. Progressives are installing solar energy panels to reduce reliance on fossil fuels and are proponents of developing more sources of alternative energy. Environmental activists ride their bikes to work and support public transportation.

Meanwhile, conservatives are still driving around in their SUVs, lobbying for more offshore drilling, and denying global warming even exists. It is their philosophy of endless growth and an unregulated government that has created the mess we are in.

photo by Morgan/James Photography

This is not, as the Right would have you believe, a fight between those who want to save fish and those who want jobs and opportunity for people. That is a false dichotomy. Environmental activists want a clean healthy environment that is in balance so that both fish and people can thrive and prosper. We are struggling for a world where our air is not killing our children with asthma, where the water we drink is not toxic, and where we live in harmony with nature.

Who do **YOU** agree with?

Who best represents the interests of the environment, the Right or the Left? That's easy: the Left. The Left better represents the interests of the environment over the interests of human beings, over the interests of national security and over the interests of basic common sense.

One of the complaints I have had with the Left is that they do not understand the concept that life's all "connected." Life is like a pond in which a stone has been tossed, with each subsequent ring spreading out indefinitely, touching everything in its path. Liberals believe that if they throw the same stone in the same pond, it will remain as glassy as when they started.

photo by Hart Photography

When Liberals create legislation that provides "protection" for the Delta smelt by turning off the pumps in the Delta that send water to Central Valley farmers, those ripples are felt. The record low amount of water in our reservoirs is not the result of a physical drought, but rather one created by depletion to meet the needs of salmon in the San Joaquin River and the water released for the smelt. The best part? No one knows the role pumps play in the smelt shortage or if shutting them down

being threatened by our dependence on foreign oil and the Left is not immune to this reality -- just don't expect them to DO anything about it.

The world's proven conventional oil reserves are estimated at 1.3 trillion barrels. Guess what? There is as much as 2.046 trillion barrels in the United States alone of oil shale under Colorado, Utah and Wyoming. And why don't we tap into it? The Left has placed it all "off limits." They have made it so that no one can even investigate its possibilities, let alone process it. I guess they figure we can use wind and solar power to operate our military aircraft and tanks.

Finally, common sense is a rare commodity among the Left. Take a look at an example:

> "One of the complaints I have had with the Left is that they do not understand the concept that life's all 'connected.'"

from environmental activist Dan Daggett: "I know a rancher who has managed the habitat on his ranch to such a state of health that it hosts one of the largest known populations of an endangered bird (a flycatcher). An adjacent preserve of similar habitat hosts none. Leftist environmentalists have lobbied to remove the flycatcher habitat from the rancher's management and increase the size of the preserve. A conservative environmentalism would reward the rancher for his success and empower him

Each month me and the cigar smoking dude would face off in the pages of Fresno Magazine.

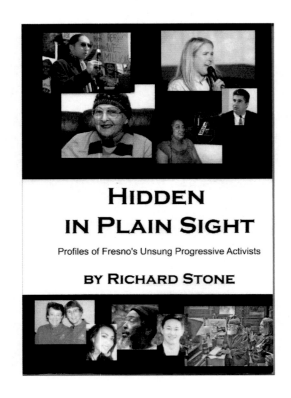

HIDDEN IN PLAIN SIGHT

Profiles of Fresno's Unsung Progressive Activists

BY RICHARD STONE

Inside the Broken California Prison System

Boston Woodard, B-88207

author talk

mike rhodes

a champion for

the homeless, journalist/photo -

journalist and former editor of Fresno's

Community Alliance newspaper, his

book, **Dispatches from the War**

Zone tells the gritty side of politics and homelessness

neglected by mainstream media.

Dispatches from the War Zone

Mike Rhodes

---

thursday | october 13 | 7pm

fig garden regional library

3071 W. Bullard Ave. | 600-4071

www.fresnolibrary.org

THE COUNTY OF FRESNO 1856

FRESNO COUNTY PUBLIC
LIBRARY

This was one of the first meetings of the Central Valley Progressive PAC held at the Fresno Center for Nonviolence.

This is a map I created to illustrate for Community Alliance readers that the people in Fresno are not as conservative as some people think.

I took this photo at one of the big immigration rights marches that took place in Fresno.

Chapter 12

A highlight in my life was being a part of the class action lawsuit on behalf of the homeless against the City of Fresno in 2007. The Federal Court ordered the City to stop violating homeless people's Constitutional rights. I won't go into great detail about it here. You can read my book for more of this exciting story. It was just so great to be able to stand up with the homeless, with competent legal counsel and stop the City from the relentless and ongoing attacks. We even forced Fresno mayor Alan Autry to do a 180 degree change and admit that his policy on homelessness was the biggest mistake of his administration.

Simone, our youngest daughter, was helpful in our effort to document the attacks on the homeless. She was interested in filmmaking and I would bring her with me to these huge homeless evictions by the city. She would have her video camera and just film away as the police and other city workers violated homeless peoples rights. It was kind of amazing how the city would do blatantly illegal things and not even care if we were filming them. Actually, that turned out to be their downfall, that they were just so callous and shameless. The things they did outraged the Federal judge and was why they lost the Class Action lawsuit. Simone filming their illegal activity was a big part of why we won.

Simone also filmed some things for me at McDonalds when a manager kicked out a disabled homeless person and would not allow her to use the bathroom, even after she had bought food. I remember the manager yelling at Simone to stop filming, as I walked up to the scene. The police were already there. I told Simone to keep filming. I thought the manager was going to blow a fuse, but Simone was undaunted.

I started getting death threats, mostly on Indymedia. Things like saying there would be a sniper that would have a rifle dialed in on me at the next event I was attending. There was another post giving directions to my house, saying I should get a more secure entry door and then someone broke into the house, leaving me a message to back off. It wasn't a written message, just the fact that they had been in my house and that they could do it again. Then there were the messages about Vanessa's location, what she was wearing and doing. Pretty disturbing stuff.

I knew that someone was trying to get me to stop some of the work I was doing, like writing articles about homelessness and other progressive causes in the Community Alliance. I did not think that whoever was doing it would follow through, but I did tell my family about it and told them if I did end up dead that they should do an in-depth investigation. Don't believe the coroner report if it says I committed suicide by shooting myself in the head three times.

What I really expected to happen, instead of them killing me, would be that they (whoever they are) would set me up for an arrest. For example, when I got pulled over for a faulty taillight on my car, I thought for sure they were going to find drugs in the trunk or back seat. No, all I got was a fix-it ticket. But, that is one of the right wings tactics - to keep you under pressure and try to stress you out, hoping that it will impact your work.

Pam and I in New York City. The whole family went when Vanessa started school there.

This photo, taken by Dallas Blanchard, illustrates the City of Fresno's policy of taking and immediately destroying homeless peoples property.

This is a photo I took at one of the many demonstrations protesting police brutality, the City of Fresno's homeless policy and an end to the war in Iraq.

Al Williams (far left), Simone and the out of control McDonalds manager.

Mike and Simone - on assignment

Chapter 13

Pam. Vanessa, Simone and I attended the World Social Forum in Caracas Venezuela in 2006. It was super exciting to be around thousands of like minded activists from all over the world. The theme was Another World is Possible. Pam and I also attended a WSF in Porto Alegre, Brazil. That gave me an opportunity to interview participants in a movement of homeless people that were taking over land, establishing farms and a distribution network. That gave me another perspective of how homelessness is addressed in other countries.

I'm a strong believer in socially conscious travel and how that can educate you by putting you in touch with things that are outside of your experience. Expanding your horizons by traveling and engaging with activists who are struggling for social change will give you a new perspective of what is possible.

In 2013 Pam and I went to Italy and spent about a week with her sister Sue and her husband Willie. We went to Naples, Rome, Florence, Venice and Cinque Terre. After Sue and Willie returned to the United States we were joined by Vanessa and Simone. We met them in Rome where we stayed for a few days, went to Livorno and from there took a ferry to Corsica. We stayed in a condo that Vanessa got (for free) through a connection she had at her job. After several great days there we took another ferry to Marseille, France. From there we went to Paris on the high speed rail. I liked everything about that trip and would do it again if I could. That is just one of those things that I never dreamed I would be able to do in my lifetime.

The next year, 2014, Pam, Vanessa and I went to Barcelona, which just blew me away. It is such a beautiful city. When we were there I was impressed with their transportation system (wide streets, sidewalks, access for bike lanes, buses and cars. A great subway system. Public art everywhere. The Ramblas! It inspired me to write an article about how Fresno could be a world class city. My first attempt at Fiction. I loved it. With any luck, that article is still online here:

https://fresnoalliance.com/how-fresno-became-a-world-class-city/

Simone and I went to Guatemala in 2014. The plan was for her to study Spanish and I was just there to make sure things went smoothly and to have a bit of a vacation. In addition to Simone learning Spanish, we had a great time. We went zip-lining in the jungle on a day that there was a storm with lightening and thunder. The people running the place did not seem concerned that a metal zip-line course might attract lightening.

Mike, Vanessa, Simone, Pam and our friend Aggie Rose in Caracas Venezuela.

Venezuela president Hugo Chavez. I took this photo of him in Porto Alegre, Brazil.

Pam and I took a side trip (from the World Social Forum in Brazil) to visit Iguazu Falls.

When Simone and Vanessa went to Cuba with the Venceremos Brigade, Pam and I met them when they returned to the United States. They walked back across the Peace Bridge in Buffalo New York. After that we went to Quebec and then back to New York. From left to right are Cody Iyall, Tony Bracamonte, Vanessa and Simone.

Vanessa and Simone in Quebec City.

This is (back row left to right): me, Bob Whalen and Willie Brusin. In the front are Pam, Mary Ann Whalen and Sue Brusin. This was on our trip to Ireland in 2011

Mike, Vie, Vanessa, Simone and Pam in 2007.

Pam and I at the Eiffel Tower in Paris and at Karl Marx's burial place in England.

Pam and I in Florence, Italy in 2013. We explored Italy with Sue and Willie Brusin (Sue is Pam's sister) and then were joined by Vanessa and Simone for one of the best vacations ever.

The family at a pool in Mazatlan, Mexico.

Mike and Pam at the southern tip of South America. We took this trip with Sue and Willie - it was a tour that took us all over Patagonia in Chile and Argentina.

Me at the KFCF 88.1 FM studio, probably being the board operator for our Street Heat or Stir it Up radio show.

This is a group photo taken after I gave a talk about homelessness at the COOL lunch (a labor group that meets once a month). That is Steve Brandau, a Tea Party City Council member, next to me. The event was packed with several City Council members and lots of police who were not exactly members of my fan club. Everything went well and I got feedback from one of the organizers that it was one of the most interesting events they ever had.

Chapter 14

After I returned to Fresno, Josh flew down to Guatemala, which eventually ended up with them getting married by a Mayan Shaman. I had almost given up on the idea that either of our daughters would ever get married, not to mention have kids. But, just as soon as you let go of an idea, it happens.

When Simone and Josh returned to Fresno Pam and I helped them plan another ceremony - one in which we could all participate in. That ceremony was held on the Fulton Mall, next to the plaque commemorating the Free Speech fight that the IWW won. The event was great, lots of family and friends attended, we had music and food and a great time was had by all.

Vanessa and Anool got married in a civil ceremony in the Bay Area and later they had a big wedding on the beach in Watsonville. In 2015 Pam and I flew with them and a few other friends on the longest flight I have ever been on. India is literally on the other side of the world. What an adventure that was! It was the biggest and most elaborately orchestrated wedding that I have ever been to. Anool rode in on a white horse, Vanessa was carried in on an elaborately decorated platform by four men and then they were married (amongst a lot of pomp and circumstance) in a huge ceremony.

To say I was impressed and blown away by the whole India wedding does not come close. It was something so far out of my experience, I'm still thinking about it. I even got to get dressed up in Indian ceremonial clothes. Pam did too. We actually looked pretty good and have photos to prove it.

For what it is worth, here are the countries I have traveled to:

All over the US
Canada
Mexico
Guatemala
El Salvador
Honduras
Belize

Nicaragua
Costa Rica
Venezuela
Brazil
Argentina
Chile
Ireland
England
France
Italy
Germany
Spain
India
Hungry
Romania
Cuba
Jamaica

Back in Fresno Pam and I were always engaged with political activity. We helped organize demonstrations in support of immigrant rights, we helped organize May Day rallies and were involved with electoral politics.

I decided to leave as editor of the Community Alliance newspaper in late 2013. At first, I think people were in disbelief that I was serious and various proposals were floated (like I should take a year off), but I made it clear that I needed to move on. Eventually we hired a new editor and over the next year or so I was able to disengage with the newspaper. I still wrote articles for the paper, but I had decided that I needed to step back.

I had been doing so many different tasks at the paper that they eventually had to hire at least three people to get the work done. The jobs created were editor, business manager and distribution manager. Five years later, even though there has been some ups and downs, the newspaper is still publishing and seems to be doing fine.

Fresno (my grandson) was born in December of 2014. I really had no idea what a great addition that would be in my life. Fresno and I get along great and I really enjoy being around him. He is like the son I never had, with the added benefit that I don't have to take care of him all the time. Now I know why everyone talks about how great being a grandparent is.

Amelia (my granddaughter) was born in May of 2017. Because Vanessa, Anool and Amelia live in the Bay Area, I don't see as much of her as I would like. Pam and I are hopeful, assuming my health is ok, that we can visit them for a week or two a couple of times a year. The house they just bought in Hayward is big enough for us to have our own room, so I'm really looking forward to getting to know Millie better.

In January 2015 my mom fell and broke her hip. I had been concerned about my mom for a while and made sure she called me daily so I knew she was OK. When she broke her hip, it had a huge impact on my life. Of course, I was concerned because she always hated the idea of going to the hospital. Surprisingly, that was not an issue for her. She went to Kaiser, had an operation to repair her hip, spent a few days in the hospital and was released to a nursing home. The nursing home did not work out and we took her home the next day.

We did better with her at her house, but life was never going to be the same again, largely because she needed a lot more assistance than she had ever needed before.

Soon after she got home and we set up a system for her care I decided to put together a book about her life. This gave me a great opportunity to talk to her, look through old photographs and some 8mm video that her dad had shot.

I got to know my mom in a much deeper way and will be forever grateful that we had that time to talk and share stories. Eventually I produced a photo book of her life, several video interviews with her talking about her life and I digitalized the 8mm video her dad shot.

Eventually she needed to move into a residential care facility, we fixed up her house and Simone, Josh and Fresno are living there now. Fresno is growing up in the same house that I grew up in. In fact, he sleeps in the same bedroom I was in at his age.

While I'm really satisfied with having been able to interview my mom and get her life story told, I really wish I would have done that with my grandparents and great grandparents. Every person's life is important and is worth writing about. That is why I feel extremely fortunate to have this time right now to reflect on my life.

While you can never tell everything about your life in a writing project like this, there is value in sharing what I feel was significant in my life. It almost goes without saying that this is from my perspective and I'm sure that other people who were there (with me) at the same time will see things differently - from their own point of view. That is to be expected and I think it would be interesting to have their life stories told so you could compare and contrast and hopefully come as close as possible to a balanced view of what actually happened.

Unfortunately, I can't include everyone else's viewpoint in My Life's Story (which I think would have made it more interesting). In the end, this is my best insights into what happened in my life. I can't guarantee that everything is 100% accurate, but I have no reason to give you anything other than the truth, at least as far as I understand it.

I sure don't know what my future holds. I am happy that I have had the time to not only live this life, but also to be able to write about and reflect on the significance of my life, the influence I might have had on others, and what impact it has had on the world around me.

I found out about my diagnosis of 4th stage lung cancer in January 2018. I went to the doctor complaining about a pain in my hip. I thought it might be arthritis or maybe the ball joint between my leg and hip needed to be replaced. I never thought for a minute that I might have cancer, because I was otherwise in good health and had no other symptoms.

The diagnosis of maybe having a year to live was a bit unsettling. Everyone knows they are going to die, but being told that you have a specific and limited time to live will get you thinking.

Kaiser wasted no time in getting me on a treatment program. First was the radiation to address the cancer that had spread to my bones. That was pretty intense and was followed by full brain radiation (yeah, it had spread to my brain too). The only good news I got was that because of the genetic makeup of the cancer and my body I was eligible for Katruda, a new immunotherapy. The Katruda is meant to give your immune system the ability to identify and kill the cancer.

As I write this I am in the middle of this treatment, but I now know (July 2018) that the immunotherapy is working. The size of the cancer in my lungs has bee reduced by a third and they can no longer detect the cancer in my brain.

My friends have been very kind and have offered to help in ways that I wouldn't have imagined. Of course, I get a lot of advice about what to eat, not to eat, what supplements to take etc. I have been given enough marijuana to choke a horse (apparently people think that pot will do away with the cancer or maybe they just want me to die happy). I have been advised to fast, take LSD, and to use a hypnotherapist. A very competent Holistic Doctor has given me free advice.

In addition to the advice, I have been surprised that a couple of people have approached me about establishing awards and grants in my honor. One project is to set up a fund at the San Joaquin School of Law to benefit law students that have an interest in defending the rights of disenfranchised groups, like the homeless. Steve Malm and Howard Watkins are working on that. The Community Alliance has set up a Mike Rhodes Writer's Award. I gave the first Award to Richard Stone at the Community Alliance fundraiser in June 2018.

Vic Bedoian did an oral history with me at KFCF. So, my health situation has motivated a number of people to move on some projects that would not have been started if I did not have a health crisis. I think all of the attention is sweet and I appreciate all of their efforts.

Also, I did set up a Health Blog at http://mikerhodes.us/health-blog/ which should still be on the Internet for years to come. Some of the comments on that blog are just great.

I will conclude by saying that whatever the outcome of this battle against cancer, I have lived a good life, I look forward to every day in front of me and it was an honor and a privilege to find love and to have lived a meaningful life. Thank you for sharing this journey with me.

This is me and my mom in 2016 on her 84 birthday.

This is my mom with her cousin Marilyn Bopp visiting at my mom's new home. I recently found out that Marilyn's son Erik bought the Residential Care Facility where my mom lives.

From left to right: Pam, Mike, Simone, Vie, Fresno, Josh, Vanessa and Anool in our 2015 holiday photo.

Simone, Pam and I in the front row at the Fresno Fairgrounds to hear Bernie Sanders in May 2016.

Simone and Josh's wedding on the Fulton Mall.

Simone and Josh were married first in Guatemala by a Shaman and then on the Fulton Mall in downtown Fresno.

Group shot at Vanessa and Anool's wedding in Watsonville.

Vanessa arriving at her wedding in Indore, India. This was the culmination after days of ceremonies - Indian weddings are incredible events and I was honored to be a part of it.

Anool (Vanessa's husband) arrived on this white horse that was part of a parade with music and dancing down the street that led to the wedding.

Mike and Pam all dressed up at Vanessa's wedding in India.

Lucky (Anool's Dad) and Mike dancing in celebration at the India wedding.

Me and my grandson Fresno. We always have a great time together.

Amelia is the newest addition to our family. I hope I have time to get to know her as well as I know Fresno.

June 2018 at Sabrina's graduation party. From left to right Willie Brusin, Sabrina Desha (the graduate), Sue Brusin, Simone Cranston-Rhodes who is holding Amelia (my granddaughter), Pam Whalen, Joel (Raina's boyfriend), Raina Desha, Tania Brusin Desha, Kirby Desha, Morgan Prillaman , Athea Brusin-Prillaman, Mike Rhodes, Vanessa Rhodes and Anirudhasingh Sodha.

I have always enjoyed gardening. Usually I grow tomatoes, eggplants and peppers but other times I try to expand my horizons by giving more exotic herbs a chance to grow in our garden.

Made in the USA
San Bernardino, CA
26 July 2020